An Accountable American

www.anaccountableamerican.com

An Accountable American

Copyright 2020 by Lisa Ann Feeley

$18.95 US

All rights reserved. No part of this book shall be reproduced, stored in a retrieval system, or transmitted by any means, electronic, mechanical, photocopying, or otherwise, without written permission from the publisher. No patent liability is assumed with respect to the use of the information contained herein. Although every precaution has been taken in the preparation of this book, the publisher and author assume no responsibility for errors or omissions. For general inquiries about An Accountable America or to contact the author, please refer to our website: anaccountableamerican.com

International Standard Book Number: 978-0-9743159-2-8
First Edition: Printed in the United States of America, September 2020

Note: Reasonable care has been taken in the preparation of information to ensure clarity and accuracy. The book is based upon the author's personal experience as well as professional experience. The author specifically disclaims any liability, loss or risk, personal or otherwise, which is incurred as a consequence, directly or indirectly, of the use and application of any of the contents in this book.

Cover photos: Constitution © Depositphotos.com/alptraum Flag on fence © Depositphotos.com/cfarmer
Copy editor: Beth Brown and Jeff Shelton
Website Designer: Charlton Consulting
Cover Designer: Tamara Dever, TLC Book Design, TLCBookDesign.com
Graphic Artist: Sydney Dunn Photography

An Accountable American

Journey to Accountability

Our America Today		1
Helpful Definitions		3
Author's Note		4
Personal Accountability Pledge		11
Lesson 1:	History, Metrics, and our Future	14
Lesson 2:	The Fundamental Factors	36
Lesson 3:	American Stories from four Accountable Americans	62
Lesson 4:	Fate. Faith. Grace. Choice.	80
Lesson 5:	Your Mindset Matters	100
Lesson 6:	Mindfulness and Empathy	106
Lesson 7:	Asking better questions	114
Lesson 8:	Creating a Success for All Movement	124
Lesson 9:	Everyday Accountability	134
Lesson 10:	Putting Accountability to the test	142
Acknowledgments		168
Appendix:	Circle of Influence / Scorecard November 3, 2020 – The Choice The Pandemic and Civil Unrest Works Cited	169 - 187
Author Bio		188

Our America today

As this book goes to publication, I want you to picture this in your mind:

- An estimated 2,000 American cities and towns with protests and civil unrest (this is almost 10% of all cities and towns in our country)
- Approximately 700 police officers injured
- 29 lives extinguished (several children) stemming from the protests
- $1.4B in projected damages/total losses to local economies (from destruction of personal and business property / lost business income)
- Estimated $5B over the next 10 years
- An immeasurable amount of mental anguish caused to Americans

Not a pretty picture, is it? While I wish this was not reality, these are the facts. And since we only have ourselves to blame, we now have a choice: do we sink our heads in the sand and hope by some miracle our country turns itself around or do we stand up, focus on being accountable, and solve these challenges? Let me ask you: how tired are you? What more will it take until we reach the point where we have no other choice but to change? How many more lives will need to be lost? At that point, will we have surpassed the point of no return?

My response and my call to action is this: be emboldened for change now. Not one more life need be sacrificed. Accountability is needed - NOW. Sound impossible? I promise you it is not! Because there are millions of us who do care and we are empowered. Remember, we are a sovereign people. We govern ourselves – even though we delegate our sovereign power to elected officials - our government originates from *We the People.*

Now, emotion is powerful but, make no mistake - without a process behind that passion to enact change and without a vision, it gets us nowhere but feeling defeated. Remember, to reach critical mass in any movement always starts with one person, a process, and a vision. That's what I am offering in this book.

What can you do to help? Do your part to become accountable. Are we going to agree on everything? Of course not. But, as a nation, for over 200+ years, we have been able to find a way to do the right thing and we always, as a general rule, had a good barometer for what was wrong. I am confident there is a better path forward. We just need to take those steps. Let's get started. Join me in a new movement. A movement that includes all lives. A movement of positive action that will result in incredible outcomes for all Americans. A movement that is designed and implemented by each one of us *– for ALL of us.*

Helpful definitions

pro·cess - noun - a series of actions or steps taken in order to achieve a particular end

the·o·ry – noun – a system of ideas intended to explain something; a set of principles on which the practice of an activity is based; an idea used to justify a course of action

Lean Six Sigma – combines a culture with a data driven methodology which focuses on reducing errors / mistakes, increasing efficiencies, creating knowledge, and resulting in a process that delivers value. Lean Six Sigma provides a framework for overall culture change. *A Lean principle is to be in the constant pursuit of perfection.*

ac·count·a·bil·i·ty – noun - the quality or state of being accountable; an obligation to account for one's actions

fact – noun – a thing that has proven to be true

fic·tion – noun - an assumption of a possibility as a fact irrespective of the question of its truth

choice – noun – an act of making a decision when faced with two or more possibilities; the power of choosing

sto·ry– noun - a statement regarding the facts pertinent to a situation

Author's Note

This book is about inspiration and leadership. Leading yourself; then, helping to lead others. The strategies I propose are aimed at providing motivation and positive guidance to lead you, the reader, to a path of achieving enlightenment, peace, and prosperity. It lays out my ***Theory of Accountability***. It provides steps I have used as my personal roadmap, blueprint if you will, for achieving what I have defined as success. While you may be tempted to pick and choose which ones you want to implement, I would suggest that this blueprint can be compared to a recipe for cookies – while you might be able to substitute a few items (raisins for chocolate chips), you can't substitute the main ingredients (baking soda for baking powder) or you won't have nearly as much success.

However, a life journey, as you might imagine, is personal so each fundamental should be adjusted to work best for you. No one can really know more about you than you. The book is structured via "lessons." Within some of the lessons, there are some exercises for you to consider completing. In addition, you will find at the end of each chapter Steps to Betterment which bullets the key takeaways from each lesson and tips to parents of children and teenagers. For future reference, you can just review these sections if you like.

Gratitude is owed to the many who guided me along my path. From their wisdom, I was able to establish a system of fundamental steps that when connected with each other resulted in achieving accountability. By being accountable, I was able to secure a life of enlightenment, peace, and prosperity. I am writing this book because our country is suffering. We have changed as a country dramatically, and not for the better. As a comprehensive community of 330 million Americans, we have become less accountable over the past forty years. This lack of accountability is resulting in significant societal challenges and civil unrest. This book is my contribution to Americans who are seeking change, whether it is to better themselves or to help others become more accountable. May the lessons provide the desired outcomes you are seeking.

I acknowledge that the strategies may not address all the challenges which unfortunately exist for some of my fellow Americans. However, the readers who successfully implement at least most of the steps can increase the chances for better outcomes. Since the beginning of time, unfairness and inequities have existed – it is not just an issue for our country, but for many countries. These concerns persist for many reasons of which no one person can resolve. As long as free will exists, poor choices will be made. Bad outcomes occur, laws are created, and systems are put in place that might address but a portion of the problem but not all.

Many of the systems in our country have also been designed by people for which no accountability was put in place. In hope that most Americans desire to seek more positive changes in their lives and the lives of their loved ones, communities, and their fellow Americans, I am presenting a way to get us started. Considering there are an estimated 250 million adults (ages 18 and older), can you imagine what we could accomplish together if each of us committed to a path of accountability? If when we made decisions, we did so with the intent of being accountable for all our choices and we made those choices with the intent to ensure a better America for generations to come.

Assumptions are not generally a good practice, but I am going to assume if you have picked up this book, you have feelings about the topic of accountability. It is certainly a hot topic in today's world. Most people that I have met in the last few years would agree that we do not have enough accountable people. We likely agree that teaching more people about accountability and helping them enact the process to becoming more accountable would be a positive for everyone. Please allow me to share a little about my personal life journey.

At 19, I first got a glimpse into my "personality style" during college. As part of our orientation to be advisors in our dorms and in an organizational behavior course, we were given a personality profile assessment called Myers Briggs Test Indicator (MBTI). Maybe you are familiar with it. Like most personality profiles, it identifies characteristics/traits based on your responses to a series of questions. If you are not familiar with it, it was quite an interesting exercise and I would suggest looking into it if you are interested in learning more about your style which can help you get to understand yourself better. Suffice to say, I am the quintessential ENTJ.

Let me explain a little more. An individual whose profile results indicate an "ENTJ" style means this person is someone who possesses (e) extraverted, (n) intuitive, (t) thinking, and (j) judging as their key personality traits. According to significant research in the field of personality assessments, this profile is attributed to only 1% of all women in the U.S. and about 2.5% to 3% of men. Now, you could be thinking, that this is either good news or bad news. Here is my personal perspective and interpretation: it explained a lot of how I had lived my life so far.

Having grown up all over the U.S. and in a few countries being the daughter of an Air Force Pilot and serial entrepreneur Dad and an outgoing stay at home/co-entrepreneur Mom, my choice at a young age was I could either crawl under a rock and be mild, meek, and shy, or try to make friends everywhere I went. It seemed more fun to choose the latter. I now, thanks to this MBTI assessment, understand why. It was my "Extraversion Trait."

In addition to extraversion, the "intuition" component explained why I so often looked to the future and not so much the past, and while, I do enjoy my facts (which is a sensing trait - the opposite of the intuitive trait), I am more of a thinker and problem solver and am very interested in what is possible. The "thinking" and "judging" traits or preferences are most definitely right on target but to be honest, I consider the "t" trait to be more an indicator of the fact that it's opposite of the "feeling" trait which I most definitely missing. Most of those characteristics of someone who favors the "feeling" trait involve trusting your heart and being more emotional. These individuals make decisions using their heart vs. those of us who have the "thinking" trait which means we make decisions from logic and believe in explanations from a point of cold hard truth vs. tact.

The "thinking" trait that best identifies my approach throughout my life is that I make decisions with my head and believe that truth is more important than being tactful. Now, my loved ones will share with you that it is easy for me to do because they are not sure I know how to use my heart… but in fairness, over time, I have learned to use it more the older I get (I think). Lastly, the judging trait or preference is as strong as my extraversion trait. It means that I prefer a planned and orderly way of life.

<u>Bottom line</u>: my interpretation is that I have come to learn that I am a control freak. I admit it, I am a self-proclaimed triple Type A personality. One that does not believe in stress (though my husband says I have no stress because my strategy is to unload it on everyone around me). After thirty-one years of marriage, I will say his sense of humor is one of his best traits…and I will leave it at that. For those individuals that know me well, they are likely laughing and are in full agreement with this assessment.

For those of you who are not familiar with the different types of personality assessments, I have enjoyed participating in them as they provide some good insights to consider. They provide insights on your preferred approach to addressing tasks and maybe why you do some of what you do. Knowing this information can be helpful because you can choose to work on being better at something if you know what your tendency is (ex: I know I need to work more at being sensitive to individuals who are introverted in order to more effectively communicate).

Throughout my career, I have taken the MBTI at least four more times. I still have the preference for ENTJ so even though I embrace change, I guess I am who I am. It was also interesting to learn that the majority of senior business leaders in America's largest companies share this personality profile.

In researching the traits of how to be a more effective leader, I have learned that the ENTJ personality style can often be challenged with a lower Emotional Quotient (EQ). This means we might need to learn to better empathize with others. Doing so is helpful when collaborating with people of other personality styles. (We have no problem, apparently, getting along with other ENTJs). With my low "feeling" trait, I must work hard at having empathy and compassion.

In summary, I share this information because when you combine my ENTJ style with my 35+ year career background in finance, sales, entrepreneurship, and teaching (specifically as an instructor of Lean Six Sigma, a process efficiency methodology), I hope you have a clearer picture of why I thrive on being accountable and am passionate about helping others to realize their life goals - albeit sometimes "in a consistent, straight forward" and likely cold hard facts approach.

Over the next 200 pages, I will share the details of my theory of accountability. Unapologetically, I am passionate and dogmatic about creating the best process to increase opportunities to result in the environment we need in America for the majority of Americans. I want all of us to achieve enlightenment, peace, and prosperity. Before we begin, it is important to share the foundational belief that we each have a responsibility in making our country what it is. In order to create the change we need, our mindsets must be open to learning. God gave us each freewill, and with freewill, there will always be choices. When there are choices, there will always be good and bad choices. We will all make mistakes.

What I believe being accountable truly impacts is the choices we make. Helping people realize the foundation they need to create in order to learn and execute the process of making the best choice for himself or herself and how that can translate into the best interest of all Americans is the ultimate goal. This book is for all Americans who are looking to help America improve by doing their individual part for the best outcomes for our nation (and obviously for ourselves!). It is my purpose that through these lessons, people can get beyond what has happened in our country's past (though we still need to learn from history so as not to repeat it) and concentrate instead on what it takes to create a better future.

Staying future focused versus looking back (especially if you have had some negative things happen in your life) is more hopeful as well – you have more control over what is to come than what has already happened. What I have discovered in my 56 years is the more one seeks facts and delineates facts from fiction and negative opinions (what I have come to label as noise), the more likely one can develop the foundation needed to becoming accountable.

In other words, if you don't dig deep enough and verify all the information that is coming at you from many outlets (social media, tv, radio, etc.), you are likely going to have difficulty differentiating between what is accurate and truthful and what is a bunch of baloney. The foundation of which you are trying to become accountable, therefore, will be built on sand – not rock. Sand is not an effective way to build a life of enlightenment, peace, and prosperity.

The greatest success that could come from this book would be that thousands of Americans (ideally, tens of thousands) will be motivated to embrace these fundamental building blocks to achieve accountability and get our country on a better path forward for all Americans. I hope you agree that while our country will always experience some change (as we add more diversity and grow), we, as its citizens, need to make sure that we retain our country's founding principles and moral fiber in order to continue to exist as the incredible democracy we were meant to be. The biggest threat we face is our own inaction and our own choice to be unaccountable.

Many of our neighbors and friends have not been taught the essence of our Constitution; therefore, they are lacking perspective of what it means to be accountable. They do not understand the actions that they have taken are in stark contrast to the very principles for which our country was founded. Remember united we stand; divided we fall. Now is the time to start making changes. We need to celebrate our nation as it is the only place in the world where humans can have such freedom of choice. It is a choice. How will you choose to hold yourself accountable in order to raise the bar to realize your full potential? America is waiting!

My personal accountability pledge:

I am dedicated to being accountable. I will be intentional in my civility towards all Americans. I pledge to be empathetic and compassionate in aiding others in their journey to become more accountable. I pledge to separate my life and world view from any individuals who thrive on divisive attitudes. I will prioritize choices that target positive outcomes. I will live a life that embraces being a positive role model (i.e. a wife, a mother, a sister, a daughter, a community member, a colleague, a child of God, and a mentor). I will focus on leading and guiding myself to achieve my life's purpose and to support all my fellow Americans who wish to achieve accountability and their purpose in life.

I pledge to accept full accountability for the choices I make and understand that while life has its ups and downs, I can only do my best with the hand I have been dealt as no human can control everything. Through accountability, I choose not to blame others for the outcomes in my life when my choices have impacted such outcomes. I will be happy for others when they succeed. Life has never been and will never be a zero-sum game (where someone always wins and someone always loses). We absolutely can ALL win because we each can define what winning is!

It is my desire and hope that all readers will engage in this exciting journey; a journey of growth, a journey taken one day at a time, step by step. A journey that can result in happier journeys for future generations of Americans. It won't be easy, but I promise you, it will be worth it. The question is will you join me?

Lisa Feeley

12 An Accountable American

An Accountability Audit

To me, being accountable means...

I choose to be accountable for (who?)...

What I value in my life is...

My Talents and Unique Gifts are...

The goals I want to accomplish in the next year are:

Lesson 1:   History, Metrics, and our Future

History of the word

The word accountability comes from a French word acont and initially pertained to counting money. Over time it became associated with value as in the value of your contribution or work. So, when you choose to be accountable for something, it demonstrates your contribution and value. You are agreeing to have others "hold you accountable" to deliver whatever was promised.

The word itself is 270 years old – first used in 1750. Merriam Webster defines accountability as an obligation or willingness to accept responsibility or to account for one's actions while the Oxford English Dictionary states that to be accountable is a liability to account for and answer for one's conduct, performance of duties, etc.

My take on what being accountable means? Do more than your part. Beyond doing no harm, do good. The buck stops with you, no one else. Deliver value in exchange for the freedom of living in this incredible country. Do not blame others, ever. Make no excuses for failure. Learn. Grow. Choose enlightenment. Choose peace. Choose prosperity. Sustain this competence for your entire life. It is simple, but not easy. Making your way to becoming accountable is a journey. It is up to you to recognize the signs as to what personal development looks like for you and how you can learn from mistakes.

Our History

Researching the history of whatever I am trying to learn is as important on planning my future. Here is why. We must know what happened in the past so to understand context and to make sure we are not repeating mistakes. Understanding something's origin gives you a broader perspective. It gives you a bigger

"Luck is what happens when preparation meets opportunity"
- Seneca, Ancient Roman philosopher

picture. With regards to studying accountability in our country's history, while we made many mistakes, we have come a long way; we have learned from our past.

The first Americans to fully grasp and put in place what it meant to be accountable were the individuals that came to our country seeking a new way of life and our forefathers who were engaged in drafting our Constitution. The Preamble as the prologue for our constitution beginning with "We the People" is very effective in providing a detailed outline for the main purpose or goals of our constitution.

As you think about our country today, how do you think "We the People" or our leaders in Congress are doing in carrying forth to make sure we are still on the path of maintaining our Constitution's purpose? How do you think each American is doing in contributing to our purpose? When you consider what it means to be accountable, the below points are what I suggest you remember because when it all comes down to what we can each do individually. This is where we, actually have some power. Remember, we elect our leaders.

GOALS of the Constitution:

1) Form a more perfect union

2) Establish justice

3) Insure domestic tranquility

4) Provide for the common defense

5) Promote the general welfare

6) Secure the blessings of liberty to ourselves and our posterity

Through the establishment of our Constitution, our forefathers set out to build a comprehensive plan from which our country's people could build our lives. It is my perspective that they did their best at the time. Personally, I am quite thankful that this was completed back then because I cannot imagine what it would take today, in today's very political environment, to achieve the same feat. Was it perfect? No. Have we updated it? Yes.

As an American people, while we have had numerous periods of challenges, history has shown us that we can prevail through bad times but we have done so most effectively ONLY when the majority of Americans are willing to unify and collectively change themselves in order to create long lasting transformation to the social ills in our country. As I hope you will agree, while we have grown tremendously as a country, and have corrected some of our past wrongs, we will continue to be a work in progress. Knowing our history is an essential input to us moving forward productively because we must always remember our founding principles so as not to lose our purpose and our vision.

The failure of many Americans to have a strong knowledge of our country's history is of concern to many Americans. History, through the last twenty or so years, is being depicted inaccurately by unaccountable Americans. Consider why with as much positive progress as we have made (in the past 40 years) in regards to the acceptance of becoming much more diverse as a nation and having come through a period of such remarkable economic, social, and technological transformation, are so many Americans, like myself, disenchanted with where we are today?

Why and how have we become so very divided? These are the questions to internalize and reflect upon as you decide whether the strategies that I propose in this book might help each of us to contribute to generating sustainable positive change in our country.

In reviewing our history's past civil unrest, it is quite telling that throughout our early history during several of larger protests, i.e. the Boston Tea Party, there were actually no deaths and little violence. If you look back at other significant protests throughout the 18th century, you will find the majority of them to look very differently than today's "peaceful" protests.

As recent as the 1960's, which was a very active time in our history for marches, protests, and riots, there was more unity for the causes our parents or grandparents were protesting – though clearly some were violent, they still were not as violent or economically damaging as in recent history. In turning to the 1980's, one can't help but notice a period of very few protests. While for those of us who were growing up during this time might be thankful, it begs for an understanding of why this period was so very different?

Reflecting on how America is today, I propose there are three "big" differences to consider from our past:

1) Our country's leaders were undoubtedly more civil and more unified regardless of their political parties. There were numerous times that we had bi-partisan agreements. Today's political environment in our country stands in deep contrast to the environment of thirty years ago.

2) There is tremendously more negative rhetoric coming from our political leaders – on both sides of the aisle.

3) Our news media, with few exceptions, no longer reports news. The "news" report has become bias opinion.

Understanding that there are likely hundreds of additional factors, these 3 factors above demonstrate significant differences in the level of accountability as a fundamental competence which provides a plausible causation many of our social ills. The buck must start and end with us – as individuals. We have allowed ourselves over the last thirty years to be duped into becoming less accountable. The result to our country is considerably more violence, more unnecessary deaths, and more poor mental health issues, and more economic loss due to numerous reasons but mostly due to the destruction of property than any other time in our 244 year history. Can we do something please to change this? I know we can!

In a recent article, The Atlantic denoted that American political society has become significantly more polarized since 2010. I would submit that every American needs to take a hard look at how each of us lives our lives and acknowledge that we, collectively, have individual challenges that we must address. We must acknowledge that we have the control and the power to make most of the changes.

Let's take our media industry for example. Look at specifically, how we now receive information about "the news". The news that we are receiving today (whether written, digital media, radio, etc.) is for the most part unacceptable if we want to become a more accountable nation. I say this because, regardless of your political perspective, it is simply no longer news that's being reported. News, simply put, should be about an event that happened and reported. It should be reported factually.

That's all. Opinion is what the writer thinks of the event that happened. An analysis of the event is when experts (professionals with the expertise to analyze said event) get together and review the event and draw conclusions to why and how they think the event happened. See the difference. Delivering the news has changed drastically in the last twenty years.

Think about the last news you heard or watched or read. Tell me, was it simply the event being reported? If we are going to be honest, my opinion is likely more than 90% of what comes to us from the media is not reporting only "news", it is opinion. Worse yet, bias opinion. Meaning that the reporter has a strong opinion of the topic and shares that opinion as if it were part of the event itself, as if it were fact. And the real problem is that many Americans have a hard time determining fact from fiction. You know what did not exist in the late 80's or even the 90's? Over twenty websites that have the sole purpose and intent of determining fact from fiction in the news. I find this situation results in **unaccountability.**

Everyone is most certainly entitled to his/her opinion but where we really should be spending our time protesting is against professionals who have the experience, the credentials, and the power to report the news but instead report their opinion as the news. This includes those controlling big social media companies. Do not be fooled – there is tremendous bias among many in these organizations. This purposeful effort to fool us (as an American people) is more than a slight disservice to our country and as you might expect me to point out, is unaccountable behavior. Media reports today, for the most part, are void of facts – even though they sometimes are coupled with real world events.

Considering our news choices today, whether we are trying to better understand history or learn about the day's events, I am inclined to agree with Walter Cronkite when he referred to the issues of modern day news reporting "objective journalism and an opinion column are about as similar as the Bible and Playboy magazine." Be gravely concerned that there are some Americans who believe they are receiving real news from the latter. As Americans, we need to embark in conversations with each other about the reality of what is happening in America and share facts with each other. Ignorance is not bliss. We must choose to spend the time in gaining knowledge, we need to dig deeper, seek the facts from various sources (I know it is harder than ever before), and we need to be fastidious as to what we believe and share with others when listening or watching "the news" today.

> *"Our Constitution was made only for a moral and religious people. It is wholly inadequate to the government of any other."*
> *– John Adams*
> 2nd *President of the United States*

Wow. This pretty much sums up a challenge we face today. We should appreciate and honor what John Adam's was conveying. I wholeheartedly agree with his sentiment. We are dangerously close to becoming a nation of people with decreasing morals and commitment to religion which is in direct contrast with a Constitution that is best suited only to govern Americans who are moral and religious? So, I ask you, where are we going to be in the next twenty or thirty years?

Understanding our past as we seek to implement accountability for our future is critical because without a very clear knowledge of our past, we are destined for a more difficult, if not impossible path to realizing our dreams; those that our forefathers had in mind when they wrote our Constitution.

As a problem solver (remember that ENTJ personality), I thrive on asking better questions and seeking answers. Let's look at some cold hard facts to get us started on our journey of accountability.

Metrics

In developing my theory of accountability, I conducted extensive research to arrive at what could be used as some key metrics (often referred to as performance indicators). I propose we can analyze these metrics over time. I think many will agree that there can be a high correlation among Americans' individual actions (their inputs) and the outcomes we are living through as I write this book. My theory of accountability sets out to demonstrate that our own choices (including either choosing or not choosing to be accountable) allow us to have majority control in contributing to certain inputs and creating the processes in order to impact the outcomes. My initial challenge was to identify the problems which are significant that our country faces to determine which metrics or performance indicators could be measured. Metrics cannot be ambiguous, and we must realistically have some control to the inputs that cause the outputs.

The theory being, as we change our choices relevant to these factors, they could be measured to depict that we could indeed have a chance to change our outcomes. Now, the change can be for the good or the bad depending on the inputs which come from our values and beliefs. The goal is to (through accountability) shift from negative outcomes to more positive outcomes for all of us. In other words, as you likely have heard this question asked: can we control outcomes in some way and if so, what is the best vehicle to result in the biggest bang for our buck?

From our past, we have enough factual information to know that we have the power to control a large percentage (more than we think or more than we want to believe) of metrics that over time will result in an environment that "we the people" want (I would argue need) to achieve enlightenment, peace, and prosperity in our lives. After establishing the metrics, we need to determine what "good" or "success" looks like so that we can establish a target goal or best practice. As noted, success is achieving enlightenment, peace, and prosperity.

The bottom line is to consistently measure the metrics. This is a big undertaking, so assumptions must be made. In successful project management and problem solving in my career, you begin the process by analyzing (or taking an inventory of) your current state. Then, compare that to a point in time in the past to reach a baseline of what we want for the future. The good news is there are volumes and volumes of data and analyses identifying many problems in America giving me information to start to determine what might be impactful to measure over time.

As you will see, I am presenting an example of a scorecard (page 26 and in the Appendix), identifying some metrics of our larger social challenges that have a correlation to the inputs and the outcomes. These are metrics we can impact with a high confidence level.

In the practice of accountability, it is widely accepted to establish and utilize metrics to help us assign ratings as poor, better, and best practices and right from wrong. For purposes of holding society accountable to demonstrate how successful or unsuccessful we have been as individuals in our efforts to contribute to the better good, this accountability scorecard is being presented for purposes of our discussion on accountability to highlight specific performance indicators (metrics). As we choose to change our inputs, we can either contribute to or hinder our chances to create a productive environment for which to achieve our personal goals. To further clarify, being accountable means "proving in a measurable way that decisions we choose are right" "or that "decisions can prove to be successful metrics in achieving whatever we are striving to achieve."

In many of our organizations or companies, metrics have become a form of feedback. For many individuals, teams, companies (both non-profit and for profit), programs have been implemented to provide metrics of accountability. These key performance indicators help us to hold ourselves and colleagues accountable. Can we not correlate our individual actions and accountability (or lack thereof) to some of society's largest challenges? My point is we can! I submit that every American should focus on how to be more accountable through the consideration of what they are contributing to the equation to improve the metrics. Doing so will change the outcomes.

Every American needs to value the importance of his/her talents and commit to using these talents to bring value to themselves and others; when we go to work or when we participate in helping our families and our communities. However, here is an important point to understand: it has been proven in the world of statistics and human nature, in order to most effectively and efficiently realize/achieve positive outcomes (example: goals for an entire country), we need to measure the value so as to maximize talents to realize large benefits.

My Intended Outcome: to spark emotion and passion *(inspire a national movement)* among all Americans in the desire to identify and utilize their talents in a positive and measurable way to bring value to others while also helping others to do the same. It would be through their doing so that, I believe, would result in a significant reduction of the challenges we face in our country. As I have learned from Lean Six Sigma methodologies (as I explained earlier), in order to reach your goals you want to be constantly in *the pursuit of perfection* by implementing a process whereas, our outcomes are no more and no less than a function of our inputs.

Put simply: what we put in, we get out. In the twenty years of practicing Lean Six Sigma, I have learned that once you establish a process, you must measure it (to ensure it meets or exceeds what you are desiring), see if needs any adjustment, adjust as needed and implement and control. The process should be repeatable and predictable. Once you learn and embrace accountability, it is easier to build on your habits and sustain it.

Understand that being accountable is no more than a lot of smaller inputs collectively resulting in **POSITIVE outputs.** When we become accountable, we have within our power to increase our chances at success and we then, can contribute to impacting our country (realizing of course, we are never 100% in control). It has been my good fortune to have taught thousands of individuals (through classes, webinars, and conferences) in the past twenty years in courses for developing and implementing goals, improving processes, organizational and change management, Lean Six Sigma, and more.

Through these classes and interactions with others, it occurred to me that while some percentage of the general population have set goals for themselves, we may or may not have established actual metrics with which we could regularly review to hold ourselves accountable. What I would like to focus on is the importance of measurement and how we translate our individual goals and being accountable into what could measure the success of our country's culture so as to ensure our own enlightenment, peace, and prosperity? In other words, what is the process of creating success for our ALL Americans to actually create success for ourselves?

Much like the circle of life, what we do positively (by being accountable) contributes to our circle of influence which influences a bigger circle and results in our country's environment (systems and processes) to succeed in creating better opportunities for each of us to succeed. Refer to the *Circle of Influence Graphic on page 171 in the Appendix* to ponder how your choices can impact others.

Do you see how the choices you personally make can impact not only yourself but your family and/or your community? Think of the outcomes of your choices causing a big ripple…. What are some factors you would want to measure for America's success?

What are some things we could do as accountable Americans to impact these factors?

(NOTE: Make sure that the decisions you are making every day are aligned with your values. Make sure, if you have loved ones you are responsible for, that you are clear on your expectations of accountability from your loved ones. Help them to understand what that looks like).

How can you measure whether or not you are reaching your personal goals?

What contributions are you making to your circle of influence?

For many years throughout our history, scientists of every scientific and social discipline have gathered information to give us a pretty good idea of what they believe contributes to our problems. Many of you are likely familiar with the use of benchmarks and best practices (if not, I recommend you research these tools). With a scorecard, you can track important contributing factors to assess how you are doing against goals you are trying to achieve– whether monthly, quarterly, or yearly, etc.

Establishing metrics, which many of us have implemented at work, go a long way to setting and achieving expectations. Right now, I would say (and many Americans might acknowledge) that we are paying hundreds of millions of dollars to government/leaders and not getting the return on our investment that we deserve. I am guessing we are "in the red" when it comes to our investment in accomplishing what is best for America. What do you think? Are our leaders delivering a great return?

Through years of research, learning, listening, implementing different methods and working really hard at deriving what it takes to achieve accountability (in 50 years), I believe what I am sharing as an example scorecard for just some of our country's challenges will help you, the reader, understand the concept of key performance indicators and how each of our choices (inputs) can directly impact the outcomes. Since most metrics are measured over time, I chose 1978 (when I entered high school) and compared it to this past year (2019).

As a big proponent of establishing factors and measuring them to improve and achieve goals, I propose that you reflect on your current state and come up with a plan. I subscribe to the same philosophy that Peter Drucker, one of America's great leadership gurus, has when it comes to achieving goals: "If you can't measure it, you can't improve it."

ACCOUNTABILITY SCORECARD AMERICA
for Achieving a Successful Environment

YOUR GUESS?

Significant social factors	**1978**	**2019**
% of Married Couples (ages 18 – 34)	59%	_____
% of all babies born to single mom*	16%	_____
% of babies born to unmarried parents	14.8%	_____
% of individuals ages 22 - 34 still living with parents	24%	_____
% of individuals ages <25 with a college degree	25%	_____
% of households living in poverty	9.6%	_____
% of Federal Taxes paid by Top 10% of earners	38%	_____
% of Americans with Health Insurance	78%	_____
% of Americans who believe in God	94%	_____
sub factor: **% of Americans attending church service weekly**	40%	_____

GO TO PAGE 172 in the Appendix to find the actual answers

If you do not take an interest in the affairs of your government, you are doomed to live under the rule of fools." – Plato
Greek Philosopher

As you read the real percentages on the scorecard in the appendix, how does it appear we are doing? I think the data speaks loud and clear, but it is important that you reach your own conclusion. In my review of the outcomes, I would conclude there is a significant amount of opportunity for us but we have a lot of work to do.

We need to find a way to be more accountable as individuals and to hold leaders accountable to put systems in place that will allow us to be more accountable. Obviously, we would never expect that metrics would stay stagnant as we have grown a lot and the diversity in our country has changed dramatically since 1978, however, I hope it is unlikely that many of us are happy with these outcomes.

Can we agree that it is not a positive factor for babies to be born to only one parent (we have the highest number of babies in the world among developed countries that are in this situation)? How about agreeing that it is not positive that we have less Americans coming together in faith and that we have more Americans living in poverty? In addition, we are hitting all-time records of young people not securing financial independence from their parents.

Let's consider more positive possibilities: can you see that as a more accountable nation, we might have less divorce, more babies born into stable families with two married parents, and we might be able to provide an environment for more financially independent younger citizens to achieve their dreams. If we improve these metrics, we would have less households living in poverty instead of relying on the government. How does that sound to you?

Another positive outcome would be that with more people successfully employed, and realizing the opportunities in America, more individuals would have affordable health insurance and share the tax burden among more Americans instead of only a small percentage. Personally, it is not accountable that 44% of Americans pay no taxes at all yet they are living in the same country with the same benefits as the rest of their fellow Americans. When we are all pitching in, we can all reap the benefits, and we all feel better about our contributions. While I do not profess to be a social scientist or psychologist, I have conducted enough research and studied data enough to say that beyond any doubt, the implications of these issues and of the choices we are making (or not making) are causing terrible outcomes for millions of Americans.

Here is an example of the domino impact of just one metric: With the increase of single moms, there is an increase of those living in poverty (estimated at 90%). The increase of single moms is staggering and costly in several ways to our society but especially detrimental to the single mom herself.

As accountable Americans, we must help all Americans who want to take a different route. Recently, Brookings Institute published information about this trend of babies born to single moms. The researcher summarizes "if we have learned any policy lesson over the past 25 years, it is that for children living in single parent homes, the odds of living in poverty are great." This is something we can change, but it will take time and it will take accountability.

Having been founded as a religious nation, a surprising and disappointing metric is the decrease in the belief in any formal religion and the contradictions of Americans (we seem to want our cake and eat it too). In a poll from Pew Research (taken just 5 years ago), only 48% of U.S. Adults answered that growth in Americans' non-belief in religion was a bad thing as those respondents connected being religious as having more morality. However, 50% responded that "believing in religion did not matter" or that it was actually "a good thing" that we were becoming a nation of disbelievers. **Wow! 11% of the 50% of Americans polled actually thought it would be good for Americans to not have any belief in God.**

We are a country that was founded on Christian principles. While some people will want to debate that belief in religion has little impact on morality which has no impact on accountability, I believe the argument is not based on research or grounded in past outcomes. Believing in a greater power, and/or being spiritual, in general, makes us more aware and hopefully, less selfish. As individuals with a strong moral compass, we have a better sense of right and wrong. As a parent, it would be my advice to teach faith in a belief in a greater good; a bigger power – beyond just ourselves. Our path to achieving success is not as effectively achieved when we make it a one-person journey.

Future

Any American who has pride in being American, has concern for our country, and wants to be accountable, should take the time to study and understand the perspectives and opinions of our founding forefathers like John Adams. Mr. Adams and his constituents understood all too well that morality and religion were critical components to the success of America. Religion is part of the very fiber of how and why we were created as a country. If you recall, England was not affording us the religious liberty we wanted. John Adams reminded early Americans that "our constitution was made only for a moral and religious people. It is wholly inadequate to the government of any other."

It is very compelling statement when you look at America today. It is a significant issue facing our country: how will we embrace and live the values from our Constitution that were so delicately crafted by our founding fathers who only wanted the best for all Americans if we lose our morality and direct tie to religion? How do we embrace wanting to be responsible for ourselves and our brothers and sisters and have no faith in anything greater than ourselves?

While it is possible to be both accountable and believe only in yourself, the question I put before you to consider is: it the best approach for an entire nation? Do we want to be a nation that takes that chance? We were founded on religion and the expectation that the founding fathers articulated clearly: the need to remain a moral and religious people so that we could be guided and governed by the Constitution.

This very foundation that we need to stand united is what increases our chances for success. To try to live in a nation of 330 million people selfishly and only living with no consideration of the impact to others poses a serious risk to the nation as a whole as evidenced by both the metrics above and by the tens of thousands of people who have needlessly died in the past few years alone. We will be a country more united and more successful if the majority of us is a moral and religious people who are willing embrace accountability.

We can only hope to positively impact our biggest challenges when all Americans are held accountable for their choices. If we cannot agree on this, we are putting ourselves at risk for continuing to be divided as many Americans. We must understand that when we are not held accountable, we will continue making poor decisions to the detriment of the majority as there will be no reason to change.

Let's consider an example of how the process could work to change an outcome:

What we want to impact: Reduction of poverty (goal would be a reduced %)
Current Status: Too many families living in poverty (this would be a # or %)

The input: Choices made by individuals that result in an increased chance of living in poverty (ex: choosing to engage in drugs that result in them losing their jobs, choosing to have a baby outside of marriage or stable, committed relationship that would provide financial security for such baby; choosing to live beyond his/her means putting the person in extreme debt).

What can change: Through learning to be more accountable and putting systems in place to support and incentivize more accountable choices, it is possible to change current inputs (these choices). While changing every single situation is not realistic, it is a fact that a larger percentage of individuals are making choices vs. those who do not have a choice. As a country, we can help these individuals learn to make better choices which would then, improve their chances of positive results.

New Future Outcome: More people choosing a healthy lifestyle (i.e. not taking drugs) which results in them keeping their jobs, more people choosing to wait to have a baby until they have financial security to provide for the baby, and more people choosing to live within their means and not leveraging their future with poor purchases. All these CHOICES would result in less people in poverty.

Another change that all of us can be involved in is to start choosing leaders who will bring about the necessary changes via laws, structure, and systems (including enforcing the laws we have) we want to impact. We cannot expect our outcomes to change when we are choosing to put the same unaccountable people back into their positions. We should commit to holding unaccountable people accountable. Since actions speak louder than words, we must also realize that our younger generation is watching the actions of both what we are doing as well as watching what the unaccountable "so called" leaders at all levels of America are doing. And what these unaccountable leaders are doing is allowing unaccountable behavior to continue.

What do you expect our younger adults to learn? What's worse is that we have some leaders not only failing to stop unaccountable actions but participating themselves in such unaccountable behavior all while wondering how and why younger generations are not as accountable as our greatest generation. Do you see the quandary we have created for them? Recent displays of our failure to hold unaccountable people accountable were on the news everywhere for the world to see.

This lack of action furthered more unaccountable behavior which included looting and destruction of property (from cars and businesses to historical monuments). Many Americans watched in dismay and horror as our community and national leaders and even law enforcement (following orders of their mayors) stood by while a minority of unaccountable Americans caused destruction – regardless how senseless. For example, by destroying historical statues, these individuals eliminated the opportunity for future Americans to have productive conversations. Conversations that could have very well helped our country make changes for the better. They took away future Americans' chances to understand our past. History is critically important to understand our future as I pointed out earlier. Whether positive (so that we can celebrate what we did successfully and build on it) or negative (recognize what happen), we need it to plan our future better.

Removing our history (now called the cancel culture) does not, in any way, help us achieve future goals nor drive us to be better citizens. Change starts with each of us as individuals. If you learn but one lesson about how to create a better future, it would be to have the understanding that each wrong or poor decision or each positive or good decision we make is on us as an individual. Collectively, decisions add up to either good or bad results. The words that come to mind for me are the lyrics from a song by Michael Jackson called "Man in the Mirror". If you have not heard it, it is worth googling and listening to.

It is time, as Americans, we embrace the obligation to both our creator and to our fellow Americans *to engage in living an accountable life* because it will be through this commitment and focus that we will become stronger individually. In realizing our potential individually, we can collectively have a more positive impact on our families, our communities, our states, and eventually, our entire country. Being accountable is part of the foundation of integrity. Without integrity, one cannot build trust. Without trust, one cannot build relationships and since our very lives exist to interact with other humans (all 330 million of us), life would definitely be more difficult and not as peaceful without integrity, trust, and relationships. We are social. We were created to achieve great things so long as we stand united.

STEPS TOWARD BETTERMENT

1. Be vulnerable
2. Write down what you want others to hold you accountable for
3. Make a commitment and find an accountability partner
4. Remember that accountability is a thick skin sport; you have to be willing to be honest, introspective, and transparent
5. Last, but not least, use sticky notes to put your daily motivation reminders all around your home (mirrors, cabinets, etc.)

TIPS FOR PARENTS

FOR CHILDREN:

Help them to understand how their participation in household chores are an important part of contributing to the family. In addition, if they receive an allowance, explain how they should be accountable by not spending all their money immediately. They should save some just in case they need it a little later. Young children can begin to understand how their actions can help or hurt others around them and they should begin to be taught that they will be held accountable for their actions if they fail to do something they were asked to do (i.e. make their bed, set the table, etc.)

FOR YOUNG ADULTS:

Teach your young adult about metrics. Review the Circle of Influence and share how you would answer the questions on the prior pages regarding what you believe are important metrics to measure. Have your teenager decide what he or she thinks is most important and how they can contribute to the better good. When our daughters were 14 and 15, we agreed on 12 – 15 factors/inputs that were incorporated into a contract with them. This contract began at age 15 and it terminated the day they graduated college. It was extremely effective as it allowed all three of us to clearly understand the factors and targeted outcomes. As in any contract, there were benefits to be realized when goals were achieved. Example: We agreed on curfew hours, part-time jobs/hours to be worked, grades to be maintained, participation in sports and church, etc. and in turn, as parents, we agreed to purchase a used car, match funds for savings from the part-time job, and so forth.

We can say that the agreement reduced potential arguments and both our daughters were successful in realizing their goals from doing well in high school, to securing scholarships for college, to graduating college, and securing careers allowing them to be financially independent by age 22. Did my husband and I think any of this was a guarantee because of a contract? Of course not. However, did it help each of us to have a mature conversation and help our young adult have a better chance of succeeding by having a written plan? Absolutely!

LESSON 2 – The Fundamental Factors

Realize as you learn about these fundamentals to achieving accountability that there are shades of accountability. Find what motivates you. I am asking you to at least commit to taking a first step toward accountability. As I shared earlier, I have been teaching courses on efficiency methodologies for many years. It is through Lean Six Sigma that I arrived at my Theory of Accountability. For twenty years I have been engaged in using this method both in my life and at work. Lean Methodology with Six Sigma involves creating processes that seek to bring more value through an increase in efficiencies, thereby reducing mistakes/errors to improve performance.

This practice became well known in our country in the mid-1980s and has gained significant popularity, not only in manufacturing (where many of you may be familiar with the use of Lean and/or Six Sigma) but now the majority of large healthcare systems as well as the Fortune 5000 have all embraced Lean. So, you might be wondering, how does this relate to Accountability?

Allow me to explain my thought process. Over the past forty years, scientists have proven the equation **$Y = f(x)$.** What this means is that Y (the output / outcome) is no more than a function of X (a variable/input/factor). Simply put, this equation helps you to realize the dependent output of a process given the different inputs. Remember the saying, "garbage in, garbage out?" Accountability, I am confident, is a measurable output for our everyday lives. It is controllable and predictable and can be repeatable. Thus, if we can confirm the OUTPUT / OUTCOME we desire, then, we can *choose the inputs* that it takes and control the process of which we get there (by being Accountable). This will allow us to consistently and predictably achieve success.

Now, this is a very high level summary of Lean Six Sigma which denotes that outcomes stem from a function of all your inputs. In any process, inputs are variables. Lean Six Sigma is most often applied to our working world. However, there are many

> *"Doing the same thing over and over again, but expecting different   results is the definition of insanity." – Albert Einstein*
> theoretical physicist who developed the theory of relativity

professionals who have applied it to everyday life (myself being one of them).

In this book, I am providing the knowledge to help you come up with the inputs, and I am suggesting an outcome that most Americans want to achieve (or some version thereof) is enlightenment, peace, and prosperity. It is up to you to choose to learn, choose to implement some or all of these inputs in order to create a plan so as to positively impact what you define as success. Once we are willing to become more accountable as individuals, we can impact the environment in which we live as Americans. The rising tide lifts all boats approach.

The methodology that I am referring to in this book is depicted as follows:

$$\text{Accountable American} = \text{Function} \; (\text{The input of you learning \& implementing the fundamentals})$$

$$Y = F(X)$$

$$\text{Successful America} = \text{Function} \; (\text{Americans practicing accountability})$$

$$Y = F(X)$$

Eventually, we will have more positive than negative impacts on correcting some of the wrongs in society. Becoming more accountable for yourself, helping loved ones become more accountable, implementing ways to ensure colleagues understand and embrace accountability will go a long way to eliminating the divisiveness and civil unrest we are facing today.

To have a positive impact to our country, I detail out the fundamentals of what we individually can do to become accountable so as to secure the best outcomes. You will hear from several individuals (accountable Americans) who I invited to share their incredible journeys - their path to accountability - and what it means to them. Each of them provides a different perspective from mine. Their journeys and mine demonstrate just how, even though we each took very different paths, arrived at accountability and achieved our goals. Over the course of these lessons, there are recurring themes.

All fundamental factors are connected to themes. Think of them "together" as water in a pitcher full of rocks and water. The rocks are the fundamentals. The themes (water) consist of 4 P's: Passion, Process, Persistence, and Performance.

> ## THEMES
>
> **PASSION:** for your country and for all Americans who share my love of what our country stands for – offering an opportunity to be all that we dream to be.
>
> **PROCESS:** the method in which hard work, persistence, and the ability to choose and execute the best option to maximize one's talents results in success as defined by enlightenment, peace, and prosperity.
>
> **PERSISTENCE:** Through mindfulness, empathy, dedication to the greater cause, the ability to stay the course despite those who may wish to derail you.
>
> **PERFORMANCE:** Embracing the implementation of action; the actual doing part and the willingness to measure one's performance so as to demonstrate value delivered in exchange for the talents you share.

The essential 8 *fundamental factors* (competencies if you will) that make up my Theory of Accountability are:

1) Identify VALUES: Understand what you value in life and write them down
2) Set GOALS: Make sure your goals align with your values and also write them down; revisit them annually.

3) CHOICE: Learn why/how fate, faith, and grace impact choice. Make informed choices. Be confident in your choice.
4) MINDSET: Build and sustain a growth mindset/an entrepreneurial mindset.
5) MINDFULNESS: being mindful, and empathetic; seek the truth.
6) SEEK THE TRUTH: Ask "better" questions (ones that lead to facts and wisdom).
7) ALL vs. ME: Keep in mind that individual actions impact ALL of us; we are many and one and need to stand united.
8) ACTION: Exercising your rights to maintain performance of the outcomes from the choices you made is a way to create more accountability in America, so long as you go about it in a respectful manner.

Let me say that while there is not necessarily an order to the factors, it is my opinion that without a solid understanding of what you value and without a vision of what you want to achieve, the journey to accountability would be very difficult. In addition, for my personal journey, it would have been impossible without my deep faith.

Bottom line is you have to decide what creates your very foundation. Without a base foundation that will not buckle when stress or environmental pressure comes, it is hard to stand firm. While I explained the origination and definition of the word, accountable, allow me to expand on what being accountable manifests itself into within terms of living life as "an Accountable American". It looks like waking up every day and utilizing your talents to be as productive as possible in the pursuit of your goals while NOT infringing on your fellow Americans abilities to live their life and pursue their own goals BUT actually contributing to their success as well.

To be accountable means planning your life intentionally so that you make choices that will increase your chances of having positive outcomes for yourself and your loved ones while doing no harm AND actually contributing to benefit others. While conducting research, I became reacquainted with the **7th Generation Principle of the Iroquois.** If you have not heard of it, it is a principle that was created by the Iroquois Indians. It's essence is that every decision you make today should take into consideration how it will impact seven generations into the future. Can you imagine?

To clarify, a generation ranges from 20 – 30 years. This principle, to me is an incredible philosophy. It most definitely embraces accountability. What could America look like if every decision each of us made considered the impact to not only our future but the future of our great, great grandchildren? It would be very accountable even if we could just think just one generation ahead. This will be outlined more in the fundamental of choice.

In my personal journey of seeking enlightenment, peace, and prosperity for myself, my loved ones, and for my fellow Americans, I discovered that my dedication and discipline to becoming accountable and maintaining that accountability throughout my life is, by far, the most effective path to reach your goals. Does being accountable guarantee happiness? No because life is not quite that simple. There are many factors beyond our control.

My recommendation is to approach life with passion to do what you can to increase your chances of reaching your goals. Give it your best. We only have but one life to live. This book provides lessons on how to realize your potential, but if, how, and when you implement these lessons is up to ONLY you.

While I identify the fundamentals, they are not in any particular order beyond the first two which are to understand what you value in life and set goals that align with what you value. It is important that these two steps are together because you have the highest likelihood to attain goals that are based on what is most important to you in your life, and that you write them down. **Think about what you value.**

Determining what you value and the importance these values play is highlighted more when you get to the fundamental of mindfulness later in the book. With regards to becoming accountable, goal setting is important to give you a vision to keep in your mind. Once you determine what you value, next will be setting goals. The choices you make become the future building blocks on top of values and goals. The types of goals you want depend on where you are in life right now but there is no time like the present to get started. While there is no magic method to coming up with goals, I would recommend using the acronym which suggests all goals be SMART (specific, measurable, achievable, realistic, and timely).

You have likely read research that depicts the correlation between high levels of self-esteem and self-confidence with that of being successful in school. In my experience as a daughter, mother, wife, manager, coach, and mentor, I have been fortunate to witness young adults achieving their goals more easily when they possessed a positive mindset and healthy dose of confidence. It really does help individuals in their pursuit of goals. As you strive to be accountable, don't set the bar too low. Remember, you are very capable of being exceptional.

To reach for "exceptional" might seem like a lofty goal but I always suggest shooting for the stars. There are many research studies that demonstrate that the average American will most often strive to at least meet whatever bar is set for them; and they usually will achieve it. The problem is our expectations are too low. I suggest we set a higher bar. In teaching accountability, every American should be taught by their parents that they are exceptional. That they have special talents that can be used to deliver exceptional outcomes so long as they make the right choices in life!

My advice is to fine tune your process of assessing your values and setting goals specifically. There are dozens of great books whether on goal setting, life strategies, leadership – all written by people who have been successful in life. Make sure the books match your definition of success. Then, read as many as you can. If you do not enjoy reading, find successful people who demonstrate accountability and ask them to mentor you.

Most adults who have achieved success in their life enjoy sharing their journey. Start with small goals, write them down, and share them with loved ones. Ask them to hold you accountable. Whether you are 15 or 50, it is always more likely that you will achieve a goal if it is written and you have shared it with someone else. If you look up a Harvard Business study about goal setting and attaining those goals, it found that ten years following graduation, the 3% of the MBA students who had written their goals down earned ten times as much as the other 97% of the students who did not write their goals down. That's impressive!

Maybe you are wondering, how can you know what your goals should be if you are a much younger adult or just starting out in your career? My recommendation is to start with what you are passionate about, where you can use your talents and take one step at a time. The following example is an exercise I have seen result in a positive impact with all ages (middle school through middle age). Get an empty poster and a marker and look to the next page.

Your Life Exercise: On one side of a poster, write down 3 – 5 answers for each of the following categories and on the other side of the poster, draw a graph depicting a timeline that starts with your current age and ends at 70 (refer to example of the graph)

FRONT OF POSTER - QUESTIONS

I think my purpose in life is to:

The following can/do have impacts on my life (positive / negative):

My talents/strengths:

Areas to work on:

What makes me happy:

What makes me sad:

What I fear:

Who / What I treasure most:

What I value:

What is important to me:

What could derail my goals:

BACK OF POSTER - TIMELINE

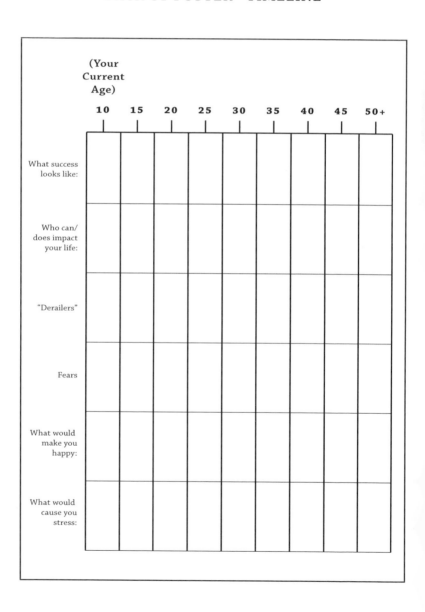

An Accountable American 47

EXAMPLE POSTER
(PARTIALLY COMPLETED)

I think my purpose in life is to:
    Be happy, make memories, make a difference

The following can/do have impacts on my life (positive / negative):
    My parents, my siblings, world affairs, money

My talents/strengths:
    Math, Art

Areas to work on:
    Communication, Education

What makes me happy:
    My hobbies, My family, My friends

What makes me sad:
    Losing a loved one

	10	15	20	25	30
What success looks like:	Doing well in school	Good grades, religious	Abstinence, College	Getting married, Traveling	Working, having a Family
Who can/ does impact your life:	Parents & Family	Parents, Teachers, Friends	Friends, Teachers, Bosses	Partner, Bosses	Partner, Children
"Derailers":	Friends move away	Doing poorly in school	Not getting scholarships	Losing a partner	Losing a job

There should be a correlation to the words written on the front of the poster and the goals written down on the back of their poster. When the poster is complete, it is much easier for each person to start putting together smaller steps that can be taken to achieve their goals in the timeframe that is written down. Obviously, life happens; goals and timelines can change but this provides you with a starting place.

It is much clearer to consider and understand the choices to make. If wrong choices (those which are not aligned with their values) are made, it is likely to derail the plan. If this happens, adjust your plan and keep moving forward. I suggest to anyone completing this exercise that he/she get a pad of paper or journal book and when so inclined, write down the steps and strategies that will get you to the FIRST GOAL.

Use words that compel action. Action words that help you move forward. In talking with hundreds of individuals who I believe have achieved enlightenment, peace, and prosperity in their lives, it is clear to arrive at the conclusion that intention, mindset, attitude, and perspective were all factors that they embraced in a positive manner. These words enabled their action. They immediately convey a call to move forward. For example, if I say to you, it is my intention to …. you immediately think about what comes next that I am expected to do.

As you know, there are things in life that we can control and things we cannot control (remember our fate discussion). Life is about trying to maximize positive outcomes. And while life cannot be lived without some risk or taking chances, an accountable individual knows how to limit risk.

While God has given each of us talents, freewill, and a limited timeframe to create our individual legacy, it is truly up to us to implement a plan that benefits as many people as possible in order to create a positive legacy that outlives us.

With this philosophy for my life, I determined what I valued, set goals, and developed a plan. I discovered along the way that while the plan has to be flexible, being accountable does not. In looking back on my life, I had to learn how to embrace the hand I was dealt, maintain my faith, be appreciative of God's grace, and make sure I gathered information before making choices.

As I am certain you will discover, becoming more accountable likely means changing habits or routines in some way. Change is never easy. In addition to wanting to change and arriving at steps in order to change, we must take inventory of the past, determine and confirm the current state, and finally, establish what the future should look like. What does enlightenment, peace, prosperity, happiness, and success look like to you?

Write your answers down. Hold yourself accountable to follow through with a plan.

History has demonstrated that we can prevail through bad times but not until the majority of Americans are willing to unify and collectively change the wrongs in our country. So, fundamentally, in order for an individual to be accountable, he or she must make a choice – about whether or not he / she is willing to accept an obligation and are willing to be more responsible to answer for one's decisions and conduct and the outcomes from such.

Having mentored or coached many individuals, teaching someone to be accountable often starts with understanding the difference between UNACCOUNTABLE and ACCOUNTABLE. What do they both look like in action, in our everyday life?

Watching the response to the pandemic play out and to the social injustices over the past few months provides us with plenty of opportunities to denote the differences. What actions were a display of unaccountable action and what actions were truly accountable? (refer to the charts on the next few pages)

The lack of accountability by many in our country presents us with a significant challenge. While there are many accountable people in our country, there are equally as many people who are unaccountable and it is their actions (or lack of actions) which are causing tremendous division in our country. Much like the saying that it only takes a few bad apples to spoil the bunch – that's our situation right now in many parts of our country. Those of us who are accountable must look around and ensure that we are helping everyone we know to become accountable including our leaders.

Accountable individuals have a plan to control what they can control and if all of us embraced this mindset, we would see incredible results as a nation. As you review the next few pages, consider reflecting what you believe in with regards to accountability for these issues. Make a commitment to be more accountable.

What Unaccountable looks like:

- Making choices without regard to long term outcomes
- Choosing to break the law or supporting those who break the law
- Choosing to divide people by labels
- Choosing to publicize inaccurate information to create anger and fear
- Blaming others for negative outcomes of poor choices you make
- Accepting the philosophy of being a victim
- Seeking an unequal advantage or access to anything (a job, a project, entrance into a club, school, etc.) based on any identifier (race, age, income, gender, etc.) other than your individual skills that you possess that differentiates you and can bring value
- Believing a non-human entity creates inequities (i.e. systems and processes). The reality is that humans create systems
- Depending on others for much of your financial security (after age 18)
- Believing life is a zero-sum game
- Supporting anyone (especially political leaders) who are unaccountable
- Embracing complacency
- Supporting ideologies that are comprised of the premise of blame based on an identifier and demanding a benefit that is not individually earned
- All career politicians (more than two terms in office)

"Nothing is so essential to the preservation of a Republican Government as a periodic rotation" – *George Mason*
American patriot and statesman

What Accountable looks like:

- Being productive every day by earning a living to support yourself and your dependents
- Contributing to the betterment of your family, community, colleagues, etc. (i.e. working, volunteering, involvement in your family)
- Planning for the future; setting goals
- Accepting the outcomes of the choices you make
- Peacefully enacting change in our country through lawful actions
- Communicating news / facts without opinion or political commentary; without any reference to labels or divisive words
- Making your choices with others in mind and with consideration of future possible outcomes
- Being fiscally responsible to live within your means
- Adhering to laws/rules to ensure the safety & wellbeing of others
- Understanding, accepting, and learning from mistakes
- Embracing a positive mental attitude
- Being happy for others' success
- Ignoring identifiers/labels; treating everyone as unique individuals
- Term limits (contributing to eliminating complacency)
- Choosing to embrace morality in everything you do
- Voting in elections as a knowledgeable, empowered citizen
- Supporting America's founding principles

Unfortunately, there seems to be so much negative media and less positive media. It is important to watch and listen to positive stories of how Americans come together and help each other. I highly recommend that we try to focus on the positive information we hear, not the negative. I believe if you are an individual who is trying to be accountable, you will seek the truth and research information you read before sharing it. Sharing inaccurate information does harm.

One interesting perspective that a high school teacher once shared with me is that what become facts are sometimes nothing more than widely agreed opinions. I think there is some truth to this statement. If you keep hearing information over and over, sometimes we resign ourselves to just believing it. Instead, make sure you fully vet what you hear and read, determine for yourself if it is useful information in your life.

As an accountable individual, do not just read the headlines or watch a few videos and pass on potential misinformation. In today's world of 10,000 media outlets where we are all so rushed, consider who is writing the information you are reading, why are they writing it, and determine if it is productive to moving our country to be united or is it dividing us? A friend of mine who is a senior leader of large projects has a saying that I think is so important to truly comprehend. He likes to say of the more complex projects that whatever it is we are trying to accomplish is often simple, but it is not easy. It seems simple to arrive at a solution but obviously the execution part is the not-so-easy part. I apply this same philosophy to the process of becoming accountable.

The steps I lay out are not rocket science; you likely have heard of most of them before but putting them into action in your life – now, that might not be so easy. To help you, I suggest one step at a time is the easiest and surest way to reach the goal. Many of us have multiple roles in life, we wear many hats (husbands and wives, dads and moms, brothers and sisters, etc.) and each and every one of us is unique (even if you are a twin). However, to improve our life and the lives of others, we must always move forward and learn from our mistakes. This is what being accountable looks like.

Frustration, helplessness, and perplexity at why our leaders who promised to change things but never seem to live up to those promises are still somehow in office. Having heard from thousands of fellow Americans who concur with these feelings gives me some hope that we can come together to improve our future. I admit, I am a no nonsense, want only the facts, take action, and get the job done kind of person.

I am unwilling to accept the current state of our country - not without at least making a concerted effort to contribute in any way to a more positive future. In the past year, of thousands of people I have met, NOT ONE has believed we are as unified as we could be. Every individual I have had the pleasure of meeting in the last five years believes our country is too divided. These are everyday Americans. Just like you. Just like me. They are out there working hard, doing everything they believe is the right way and still feel that the country is not moving in the right direction. We all want to find a better way to make a difference. I am convinced that the start of the much-needed change comes from a commitment to accountability. It is fair to say most Americans desire to find the good in others; to find what they have in common and not purposefully strive for contentiousness. Alas, we are in a situation in our country where the sensational and sad commentary and bias opinions attract the attention and these half-truths get passed on as full facts.

With a nation of people who likely have more in common than we have differences, why is this happening? Think about this the next time you turn on the television or radio or your social media. Do not let the negative information dictate your opinions. Think of everything we have in common: most of us have debt, we have parents, we have children, we have spouses or significant others, we have friends, we have hobbies, we have careers (some we like, some we don't), we have bosses, we have colleagues, we have health challenges, and list goes on and on… and during times of crises in our country against a common enemy, we have come together.

BUT, what happens when we are our own worst enemy? When the choices we are making are causing our own pain. Many of us aren't sure how we got here and what we can do to make a difference. Therefore, why we are having heartburn with the current state of America. For many of us, who grew up in the 70's and 80's, the current state of our country is NOT the America we grew up in. It is time for more accountability!

Remember the songs that came out immediately after 911? The message was positive - aimed at unifying us against evil. Evil took down our world trade center buildings in New York City. The songs evoked pride and passion and the words urged us to stand together (against those who hurt our country). As painful as that period was for our country, it is a period I remember with comfort because it was a rare occasion, in the past 20 years, where our country truly experienced great unity. Before 911, it was likely that we had not been that unified as a country since the end of WWII.

When each person makes positive changes, our nation will return to being a nation united. I, like many Americans, want to return to all Americans embracing their patriotism.

It is something we hold dear in our hearts – we have pride in our country and want to be a part of something bigger than just ourselves. Remember, in America, we have a dream and our forefathers wanted all of us to have life, liberty, and pursuit of happiness. If you do not truly believe that we have the best country on earth and you do not believe in these ideals, then it is time to ask yourself, what other place will make you happy? It is only when we return to embracing accountability as individual Americans will be able to secure the promises our country holds for each of us.

As a "guide" or "coach", it is my role to help you find the path that works best for you. You must identify and put in place a strategy to maximize your talents. Do not let anyone derail you. Seek the truth through authentic and empathetic conversations without regard to race, age, gender, income, etc. Remember, it is important to be positive and productive.

Listening to negative messages and thoughts that divide us by categories will not contribute to you being accountable. In addition to understanding how important having a plan to achieve your purpose is, having a timeline is equally as important. Since, as I mentioned earlier, we all have a finite time to live, live your life passionately and with a sense of urgency.

Our generation is at risk of not demonstrating accountability for the next generation. If we fail to be accountable and to teach accountability to our children and young adults, I am of the belief that today's millennials' children (our grandchildren) might not live in a world expecting humankind to actually support each other and love one another. We, as a human race, are not giving ourselves the best chance to secure peace nor prosperity if we decide that we want to be selfish and do our own thing with disregard to the outcomes and impacts of our choices. Individuals who continue to segregate others via labels are demonstrating unaccountable behavior. Understand these individuals want to keep us divided. Also know that it is much easier to be unaccountable so the unaccountable will blame others (almost always based on their political view, color of skin, age, gender, etc.) for their own poor choices and outcomes of failure rather than look in a mirror and change themselves. It is easier to claim the reason for the unaccountable person's problem they are facing is due to some form of discrimination.

Now, we all know that discrimination does indeed exist in our country; however, what I am suggesting is a more productive and accountable approach to solving a "wrong". By becoming an accountable person first (meaning get your house in order) and then, work with fellow accountable Americans to change the process or the law! Becoming a victim (by embracing a victim mindset) and buying into the media noise (as I referenced earlier) is further dividing all of us. Think about this for a minute: do you really believe it is productive to get angry, burn down a store or tear down a statue to produce positive outcomes for yourself or other Americans? Does it take a violent approach in order to change the poor choices of unaccountable people actually change their actions? Likely not.

The rhetoric that is happening in our country such as the continued use of "identifiers" (race, gender, age, etc.) by the media and community leaders further divide us by inciting anger. What's most concerning is that this approach is being adopted every year by more Americans. We are now beyond just debating whether someone is a Republican, Democrat, or Independent – which were about the only identifiers I can remember when I was in college.

Now, Americans are calling other Americans racist, sexist, feminist, rich, poor, blue collar, white collar, baby boomers, millennial, privileged, and the list goes on endlessly. For those who have lived a life void of accountability, it seems this approach to dividing us is trying to guilt the accountable into becoming unaccountable; to get more Americans to buy into the victim mentality. They want accountable individuals to fear that "we are wrong". This is not a successful approach to building enlightenment, peace, nor prosperity. It is a lose-lose strategy.

Unaccountable individuals prefer a them vs. us mentality. Please do not accept this mindset.

An accountable individual takes full ownership of his/her own choices, with no desire to be segregated. Americans who embrace the idea of accountability want to be recognized and rewarded ONLY for their own actual merits not for their age, race, or gender. Think about what would happen in our incredible country if there we were able to eliminate discussions about color of skin, disability, gender, and sexual preference. Imagine that we focus only on the competencies, talents, knowledge, and the value with which we can deliver outcomes. My being female should have zero impact on me being given a job or not, etc. Either I have the requisite expertise that allows me to beat out competitors or I do not. I choose this approach for America. I am hoping for an America with this level of accountability. We can do it!

What I am suggesting is that every American consider why we should want to live in an America in the 21st century where any of us want to be divided and identified by any label? What does race, sex, age, culture, ethnicity, religion, skin color, etc. have to do with the ability to secure the knowledge we need and succeed in life?

Why should any decision made (i.e. employment, promotions, our college choice, selection of awards, and hundreds of other outcomes) be based on anything other than character, integrity, knowledge, and skills we possess?

Lists are labels. Lists segregate and divide. Lists are always restrictive. Accountability is about empowerment. Empowering you to achieve what you want in life – not restricting you to say what you are unable to do because of a label someone assigns you or worse yet, you put on yourself. It is the job of our leaders to provide us with the right environment for us to have that chance.

The concepts in this book will help you on a journey towards a more accountable life. The more accountable you are, the higher the likelihood that you can reach your goals and secure peace and prosperity. Are there guarantees? No, however, I will take my chances having a plan for myself rather than having no plan at all. What I have learned, implemented, and experienced can be shared with others to hopefully positively impact their life. Obviously, no two lives are identical but we do know that proven processes can increase the likelihood of positive results. Regardless of your past or even current situation, you can choose your future mindset. Humans can make different choices. While you cannot control other's actions or attitudes, you can control your own.

Though mentioned earlier in the book, I think the point is worth repeating. Think about the fact that there are an estimated 330 million Americans of which an estimated 250 million are adults (ages 18 and older). **Can you imagine what we could accomplish together if each of us committed to a path of accountability?**

If when we made decisions, we did so with the intent of being accountable for all our choices and we made those choices with the intent to ensure a better America for generations to come.

Each of us has a unique story. As Americans, we are all different even though we share the title of American, we are a melting pot with our own perspectives. I have asked the following Accountable Americans to share their insights in hope that maybe some of their journeys will resonate with you and their stories will provide you with additional insight for your journey to enlightenment, peace, and prosperity.

STEPS TOWARD BETTERMENT

1. Accountability is about empowerment. Empowering you to achieve what you want in life – not restricting you to say what you are unable to do because of a label someone assigns you or worse yet, you put on yourself.

2. Be able to identify what accountable action looks like

3. Develop a plan that maximizes your talents

4. Do not buy in to a victim mentality

5. Embrace a positive mindset

6. Take full ownership of your choices

TIPS FOR PARENTS

FOR CHILDREN:

Help them to understand that what other people think or say about them is not as important as what they think of themselves and what loved ones (dad and mom; grandparents, etc.) tell them about themselves. Make sure they believe in themselves and their abilities! Building confidence and self-esteem is important for young children. Learning how to interpret and navigate others who think differently and sometimes negatively is a must have skill. Teach them to never label any other person and to not accept a label for themselves.

FOR YOUNG ADULTS:

Teenagers need to learn how to fail and move forward. Explain the lesson of "this too shall pass" (King Solomon and Abraham Lincoln). No issue in life need harbor stress for long. Explain that partaking in situations whereas they are identified by race, age, gender, etc. is not a win/win approach. These types of situations are limiting. The best way to secure confidence is to have a plan. If they have a good sense of self, it will be tremendously helpful in life. Have them complete the poster exercise and have the discussion of what unaccountable behavior looks like and what accountable behavior looks like.

Lesson 3: American Stories on Accountability

American Story - Mom, Wife, and Nurse; Weatherford, Texas

This is my journey and thoughts on accountability. It is my view on life as shaped by my personal history. I am the granddaughter of an immigrant. My grandfather came here from Italy via Ellis Island to this "land of opportunity" to make a better life for himself and eventually make enough money to bring my grandmother over and start a family. Being an Italian immigrant in New York in the early part of the 20th century was to be a target for discrimination by white supremacy and anti-Catholic groups who arrived earlier. The Italians were viewed as criminals and uneducated. They were offered low income or labor- intensive jobs and were often the focus of blame for any crime that happened. I have often been assumed to have Mafia connections just because of my heritage.

In spite of being the youngest of 12 children (10 who lived, 2 died young) from a very poor household, my father joined the military, started his own company and made a healthy living for himself and his family (I am the youngest of 4 children.) My family was not born into privilege and I was not even considered 'white" for a good portion of my youth (I have dark hair/eyes and olive green complexion with a first name of Maria in a school full of people who looked very different). My ancestors were not slave owners or even in America during the civil war, yet I am told that I should be ashamed of being born white and privileged and owe "reparations".

I grew up with gay siblings, black best friends, and personal experiences of violence and discrimination due to my gender or ethnicity and yet I have been recently called Nazi and racist on social media for the color of my skin.

I have always felt that everyone should be treated the same and judged only by their individual deeds or actions. I grew up wanting to help others and, so I became a nurse. As a nurse, I gave my pledge to help everyone with a need (regardless to any label). My "family of choice" is an eclectic group of different genders, different sexual orientations, mixed races, different political beliefs, etc. and I have always treated all of them with equal love and care.

I truly believe that every person should have equal rights and equal opportunities. Equal... not preferential because they feel they are owed for something that was not earned by them personally. If I am friends with you, it is because I like who you are. If I hire you for a job, it is because you have the qualifications and experience that best suits the job. It never has to do with color of your skin. There are people out there who will say I am a bad person or bad parent because of my political views; however, there is also a large group of people like me in this country that are equally shocked and outraged by the deaths or harassment of our citizens at the hands of a few bad police officers or other authorities (who isn't?) but are also not in support of the violent reaction, looting and rioting of the BLM / Antifa movement. Because I do not protest against something does not mean I support it. We should not make this a black and white (no pun intended) issue or us vs. them issue.

I believe change happens when we petition or vote to change policies, spread factual information and educate all people. I am of the view that everyone needs to look out for each other and it should not be the job of our government nor protesters to force us to be decent people. I feel in order for racial equality to exist and be accepted as "mainstream" or the norm then we need to stop making laws singling groups out. All people should be protected. We have the same end goals so let's stand united to work toward them instead of letting a few bad apples and politics divide us.

I am saddened by the descriptions of minority classifications shared in media today. It is not a cop who wrongfully restrained a suspect and killed him – it is a white cop and a black man or a Christian woman vs. an Atheist lesbian. Or a liberal teenager vs. a conservative "boomer". Why are we accepting labels? We are giving in to a pick a side mentality.

Many people feel that saying "all lives matter" is hate speech because we need to focus on only "_____ lives matter" right now. I disagree. Naming only one group is immediately singling them out to say their needs matter more. This is where the discrimination begins. Every minority group has an equal need to be protected from whatever discrimination is aimed at them and we as one society need to address all this labeling as the attitude of hate that it is.

While I understand the analogy that some are making with the house that's on fire is the one that needs the hose now but this only makes sense if there is only 1 house that's on fire on just 1 street but this is far from reality – there are dozens of houses in hundreds of neighborhoods in every state in our country. We cannot just put the fire out for that one house. Societal views need to change on a large scale and each person needs to be accountable for their own actions and their own house. This is where change starts. Don't do something to intentionally set your house on fire and then scream it is most important – this is just anarchy and we will all lose.

I grew up believing that ugly is as ugly does and you can catch more bees with honey. If you want to be respected, trusted and loved, then show this toward others. Become accountable, lead by example! We as a country can't force the right choices on every person. Doing so only breeds fear and contempt. Let's treat all people equally under the law and eliminate the *all* ____ *are* ____ negative rhetoric.

We should never just consider ourselves as black, white, red, yellow, green, gay, non-binary, straight, men, women, trans, Catholics, atheists, liberals, conservatives, or whatever... we are humans who share this country and it not big enough for all this hatred.

This is the end of my story. I look forward to a brighter future where more Americans will choose to be more accountable.

> *"We must reject the idea that every time a law's broken, society is guilty rather than the lawbreaker. It is time to restore the American precept that each individual is accountable for his actions." - Ronald Reagan*
> *40th President of the United States*

American Story – Husband, Dad, MSgt USAF – Retired; Dallas, Texas

Accountability is a big word with an even bigger meaning. It is an honor and a privilege to have been given the opportunity to share my journey towards accountability. My approach might be different, but the results are the same. I have achieved success, peace and happiness through the same fundamentals described in this book.

As a small child, we lived on a farm with my mom, dad and two younger sisters. My family did not have much money growing up, but my father was one of the pioneers of organic gardening, so good food was probably one of my earliest foundations. We lived in a mobile home on a 400-acre farm that bordered the Brazos River in Glenrose, Texas. One sunny day when I was almost 7, my mom, dad and I decided to get out and enjoy some sunshine by canoeing down the river after a week of heavy Texas rainstorms. We drove several miles North to rent a canoe and the plan was to end our trip on the banks of the river at the farm. That day changed the course of my life forever.

The spring of 1977 brought above-average rain falls which put the dams at max capacity. The Brazos River Authority opened the flood gates and released millions of gallons of water downstream and they did not inform the local community that this was going to be done. While we were paddling down river, we did not know a flood of water was heading directly for us. We wound up capsizing our canoe and free floating down the river in the raging torrent. I still remember trying to hold on to the top half of a large tree and watching the current rise at an alarming rate. My mom and I both had lifejackets on but my dad did not. He was ill-fitted wearing blue jeans and cowboy boots. That was the last time I ever saw my father.

My dad was a fairly well-known local artist and hundreds of volunteers showed up to walk the river banks, they showed up in boats, helicopters were launched and despite their efforts, it was finally presumed he drowned and his body was never recovered. We waited for hours, then days, then weeks for him to come walking up the hill from the river but he never came. We held a memorial service but there was not a burial nor is there a tombstone of any kind. Eventually, we moved away from the farm to the city where my mom found a job despite her lack of a degree or any formal skillsets. She was a punch card operator, hand typing holes in cards that were then read into room sized computers to program them. The year was 1977.

My mom never re-married and raised three children by herself. At the time of my father's drowning, I was 7 years old and my sisters were 3 years old and 18 months old. My mom was a saint. I grew up often filling in the role of father figure to my sisters and helped my mom wherever I could. She taught us to have integrity for integrity's sake. My mom did not have a strong connection to mainstream religion. That is not to say that we did not get exposed to spirituality or come to a belief in a higher power. It was done without the Bible telling us so and without any sense of guilt, sin or negativity towards our actions.

What my mom was unable to give us in material things, she made up for it by creating empowered adults with a strong sense of self, an innate desire for truth seeking and individuals who believe to this very day that they are capable of doing anything they set their mind to. She is without a doubt the best parent I am aware of.

The foundation of my sense of accountability comes from knowing how hard my mom worked to provide for us through her grief, loneliness, sadness, and all her struggles. She did her best to connect me with the male influences at a young age because she instinctively knew there were things that she could not give me and there were not a lot of males in my direct family line. I was in the Boy Scouts, and even was part of the Big Brothers and Sisters program for a bit but truth be told, I have been searching for examples of manhood my whole life. I still search for it today and I am 51.

What does it mean to be a man, a husband, a spouse and how do those things relate to me? These are questions I have had all my life and I constantly seek to refine them and improve them. Because I specifically searched for examples to follow, I have met the most incredible men that I have learned a lot from. I take a piece from each one and meld it to form my ideal of what manhood should look like. I learned woodworking and car maintenance from my grandfather although poverty taught me more about working on cars than anything.

I learned about money from one of my best friend's father, Roy Giliotti. Roy was a self-made millionaire that had an amazing talent for maximizing the potential of his surroundings. He used connections he made while deployed in the military to start a company importing pachinko machines (among other things). He taught me how to think about money, and perhaps more importantly, just to think about money rather than just accept what life throws at you.

In addition, my time in the military had an abundance of sources for learning. I learned about honor, duty, camaraderie, and perhaps it sounds corny, but I learned what "failure is not an option" means. The most valuable thing I learned in the military is what it means to be a part of something bigger than yourself. It is possible that I would have learned these lessons in all these scenarios, but the real point here is that I learned a lot more because I sought the knowledge. I was actively seeking to fill the gaps I knew I had.

Life is full of hardships and opportunities. What you choose to do with them is up to you. My family didn't choose to sue the Brazos River Authority for opening the flood gates because we knew this was what was required to prevent the dam from breaking and causing an uncontrolled flood downstream that could have killed hundreds if not thousands of people. I never felt a victim of my circumstance, I just sought to fill the role and in turn found a rich experience I might have missed otherwise.

I never went to college (although I could have with my G.I Bill money), never received an inheritance, and never had the luxury of my parents paying for anything once I turned 18. I started at zero, and yet I have travelled all over the world, completed a 24-year career in the Air Force Reserves, held a 20-year career in eyeglass manufacturing, and provided both of my daughters with a college education. My amazing wife of 25 years has been by my side for more than half my life which has made much of what I achieved possible, as she and I are aligned when it comes to being accountable.

We do right by our children, our family, our neighbors, our community and our country at every turn. We have seen firsthand what a life of hard work and focused intention can create. Witnessing unprovoked accountability in my children gives me pride and a divine sense that through all the hardships that are in their ancestry, the legacy of their actions being accountable is infinite.

American Story - Dad, Husband, and Senior Construction Leader; Charlotte, North Carolina

It is a privilege to recount a few life lessons that have aided me in my 58-year journey on this planet. A humble man honored to be going on 35 of those 58 years married to a 4'11 rock of a lady. I am a father of a wonderful son (29 years old) and beautiful daughter-in-law, who by the time this book is published will make me the happiest grandfather in the world.

Leaving home early in life, I am grateful for the leveling off in my later years gained through the stability of a loving marriage and a wonderful son (life got serious and accountable very early). I learned from them the importance of the word "vulnerability." When my son was young (5 or 6), I struggled with coming home from a hard day's work and readjusting my emotional thermostat into that of a patient father ready and willing to dote on a son that had missed him all day! I was driven, focused, and type 'A". I stayed frustrated with the desire to relate as a proper father, but only knew what I learned growing up (it was like looking in a mirror).

Learning to put my words on paper (yes, even at his young age) allowed me to be real and specific to both his needs and mine. If you have ever had one of those conversations that have great intentions, but goes south for whatever reason, you understand what I'm saying. I share many things on paper with my son (and that 4'11 rock) that might have been hard to say. Doing so created a level of vulnerability that I personally never had before that moment. When someone comes to me singing praise/pride of their child at work, I always ask the same question "Have you shared that on paper and put in under their pillow, where they will read it over and over and cherish it?"

My son has a box with all the notes I have ever written to him and yes, we continue the tradition to this day. Besides the level of vulnerability, I find that taking the time to write my son a note allows for accountability in my role as his father. My example of finding a vehicle to authentically express my love for my son will hopefully be a resource to him when he, one day soon, becomes a father.

As a Vice-President for a large healthcare system, my responsibility is to support the creation of environments. Environments that allow our employees to surpass their own expectations and as a team, raise the bar in our industry. I have been working in the healthcare sector for over 28 years and on the owner's side for 20 of those years. A desire to not just make project delivery faster, less expensive, at a higher quality, in a less adversarial way....but to change the industry is one of courage. Hope would never achieve such a desired state, but a philosophy of "the structure of collaboration," can and does.

Collaboration is one of two overly used buzzwords in my industry that also includes trust (we need "willingness to collaborate and vulnerable trust"). Collaboration is often seen as a moment of kumbaya and, when used in that manner, limited outcome will be achieved. Much like the discussion of lean tools versus a lean mindset. One can have all the lean tools in the toolbox, but without an environment and mindset that supports accountability, they will simply be tools of inadequacy.

Collaboration equals accountability, and accountability equals "measures of accountability". We have learned so much about what makes a project successful versus just simply making it to the finish line. Truly successful projects are more about the quality of the environment, communication, clarity of roles/responsibilities, EQ over IQ (IQ being the ante to be at the table) and keeping score with real measures.

Early alignment with robust measure of how we will engage based on "formal" expectations (conflict resolution, decision making, communication/listening, honesty/trust, documentation, and keeping score) is the foundation of accountability. The importance of formalized moments of reflection against formal measures have been presented such as the "1962 Tuckerman model". Tremendous value was shown with the simple moment of a retrospective.

This moment, taken even when you might not believe you or your team needed, drives accountability. We require these formal moments of retrospectives on all of our projects. The moments not only bring clarity to expectations and alignment, but holistically, education the group about the needs of the team/individuals. I take that same path with my personally life, multiple times a year as I pause to reflect upon my list of goals and expectations that I put on paper at the start of each year.

Accountability is hard because it takes formal action and thick skin. It takes vulnerability at all levels, but most importantly, at the leadership level. It's ok to take risk, be wrong, if the environment supports it and we learn from it; then it's actually a gift. As life goes, it's an assembly of seasons. We all have seasons, and often it's within the perspective of the individual to decide if it's a season of growing or harvesting.

For me the journey has not always been easy. Heck, I don't know that it has ever been easy…much less fair. I walked beside a very close friend with terminal cancer who stated "Fare/Fair" is where you eat cotton candy. Growing up a Navy brat was as strict as often stated. Patience and understanding of the needs were not often valued. Punishment back then was quick and stiff. Self-worth was hard to find. However, an awareness of structure from an accountability aspect was instilled forever.

Leaving home in your middle teens gives one a moment to have all the excuses one desires to push the easy button of blame. Courage, grit, and a steadfast desire to make a difference and never look back would drive the journey ahead. The ability to simply survive, and not realize until later that was not normal, is a statement all by itself. Yes, I had a chip on my shoulder, but it was one of "tell me I can't" and I will prove you wrong.

Manners, ethics, and a belief that we all can make a difference by working hard and going the extra step is the recipe. Being 110% accountable for my every action because it mattered (no safety net) proved an early lesson that helped make me who I am today. I have walked beside three of the best men who have walked this earth as they stared down terminal cancer. Why me? I hope they saw in me a man who related to pain, suffering, and the true value of life's journey. I somehow related to them and bonded at a level that was a gift that many might not understand.

I am a leader who sees technical skills as the ante on the table, and the real separator being courage and vulnerability. To visually and formally show the caring side at upper levels of leadership is a missing art. However, it is absolutely the element that will drive hard fast accountability deep into the most complicated teams. Hundreds of extremely complicated healthcare design and construction projects, over 3 billion in capital dollars spent, and millions of those in their moment of need served. The blessing of leading some of the most intelligent, talented, and giving people toward a common vision and mission. All with limited formal education, but with a passion for accountability and kindness is mind-blowing.

I could not have ever imagined when I walked out that door as young man, that I would be in the position that I am today. A position that honors me every day with the task I am blessed to have and the message that I carry. I see things differently. I am, as has been stated by others, "unique". I cherish the small stuff and love from the deepest realms of my heart and soul. I always strive to establish an environment of an accountability-mindset for conflict as it must be protected and matured. This is only done by helping one understand the "measures of accountability" to oneself and to everyone who crosses your path.

Being respected as a man of accountability, I hope, instills trust, respect, and the acknowledgement that I absolutely own each of my steps....one foot in front of the next. I am concerned as one who values not just the structure of accountability, but the desire and mindset. I must tell you that it is not a common foundation of new teams who we engage. There is something fundamentally missing in either the early years of future leaders or in the culture of the society that they mature into.

I find it interesting the excitement that happens when we engage people into an environment that values accomplishments and ownership. Frankly, I believe it falls directly in all three areas that motivate us as those who desire to make America strong: autonomy, mastery, and the desire to part of something larger than ourselves is about self-worth and the inward knowledge that you are making a difference.

American Story – Immigrant, husband to wonderful wife, father of two great children, grandfather of a beautiful two year old, brother, son, uncle, community leader and business executive; Indianapolis, Indiana

This is really who I am. All of these roles help define my identity, and feed into how I impact my environment, but more importantly how my own personal accountability makes me stronger in each of these important roles. I was asked to write my story from the lens of an immigrant, an immigrant of over 45 years who came to this great nation at the age of seven with my family. An immigrant and citizen who continues to strive daily through personal accountability practices to realize the full potential of living the American Dream.

For me, it was the early realization that my parents made selfless personal sacrifices to get to a better life not only for themselves but for my siblings and me. A life that we could not have imagined if we had stayed in India. A life and endless opportunities that we ran towards, not one that we ran away from! A realization of where my parents worked tirelessly in the early 70's, sometimes with multiple jobs to ground us in a strong work ethic, heads down hard work mentality and pursuit of a higher education as the ticket to success.

It's hard to pin point exactly when I first realized the accountability lesson as it is so ingrained into my thinking; but I'd imagine it was learning from my parents early on that we are "to account" for our decisions and actions and while circumstances matter, we can determine our own success. There will always be challenges to anything worth pursuing! For me, it's more of a mindset to change the "challenge" into an opportunity to do better. To maximize the potential within! Circumstances as they have been, (living in tenement housing for 4 years, having been through eight schools by the time I was in high school, until we found stability in St. Louis, Missouri in 1980) have formed how I have had to adapt and take advantage of situations I have been in and where possible, to create the right environment for success.

Subsequently, through college, graduate school, my early career, and even today, the biggest challenges have been learning how to prioritize decision making, discerning convenience and instant gratification vs long term goal attainment and understanding the impact of decisions made and consequences down the road.........sometimes years down the road.

I also learned by finding and emulating strong role models in my life; the lessons gained through trial and error and at times, failure. Understanding how to deal with failure, in particular, has motivated me to accept greater accountability, leading to what is now a position of greater authority and responsibility. Choosing to accept accountability as a core tenet of how I live my life and how to model such has served me well professionally and personally

Is it important that everyone be accountable? Imagine, if you will, if we really took to heart what this question implies. Just imagine that for a minute. Start with yourself, your circle of family and friends, and work colleagues. If we accepted this premise, we would not only achieve more, but likely achieve it faster, with more alignment, reduce duplicative efforts, and quite possibly eliminate the noise around us- allowing us to focus on what is important.

Personal accountability, if practiced well, which is the key - practicing personal accountability, and not deflecting it to others, the government, or to society is the path forward to realizing your full potential. If we all practiced it, we could help our nation realize its full potential. I am a realist and know that while we all will not magically begin to practice accountability tomorrow, we must begin somewhere and it's NEVER too late to start with yourself and improve daily.

However, the natural question arises: do we all have a fair starting point? No, we do not! But again, as an immigrant, whose parents likely came here with less than what people who are born here with which they have inherited through their birthright (citizenship and the benefits afforded by it), I can attest that through hard work, a focus on education, and an accountability mindset, I have achieved more than I thought possible. Much more than that seven-year old could have dreamt of when my family began our journey to the United States.

As with any endeavor, whether it is personal or professional, it's important to have a VISION, a purpose if you will, one that you believe in and can get behind. So many people have no belief system, are dependent on others to provide a map to success and go through life without thinking about anything but themselves.

A clear vison is needed. If you practice accountability, I believe a personal vision for yourself will evolve that will guide your work and your life. Then, the next step is to put together a plan, a personal roadmap of what success looks like, map out major milestones that will help define success, map out the steps and develop a roadmap to attain the right skills, don't give up and strive daily to improve.

All of this takes time and resources and no other country in the world has the resources we do. However, I sense we do not spend the time to explore and take full advantage of the resources we have. We become distracted and fall victim to easy solutions, we pay too much attention to social media, we let the pursuit of material things cloud our minds and lead us astray, and squander the opportunity the rest of the world wishes it had.

Taking personal accountability is the first step of many to more enlightenment, peace, and prosperity.

Professionally, in my role, I try to offer as much clarity as I can to my team. Followed by defining who is responsible, accountable, and authorized to complete a goal, plan, or task. This clarity allows me to hold myself as well as my team accountable. Personally, my wife reminds me of when I slip and holds me accountable through her actions. She role models an unwavering commitment to consistency and authentic communication. She holds our family to a higher standard.

A standard that we are not willing to relax on because we have established that consistency breeds good behavior and outcomes and authentic communication empowers us to grow. Recognizing and calling out our failures and successes helps us become more accountable to one another and ultimately to those around us and our community.

Lesson 4: Fate. Faith. Grace. Choice.

In providing an overview, in achieving accountability, I find that the factors of fate, faith, and grace must all be well understood because of their incredible impact to how we arrive at choice. This will be explained further as you continue reading but think about the fundamental of making a choice as the roof of a home (the last thing that goes on, right?), and fate, faith, and grace as three concrete pillars that brace your roof.

FATE

This is the part of life that we simply do not know. Fate is something we must learn to accept to make our journey to accountability easier. Fate is not in our control but through free will, we sometimes make bad choices and when something happens, we want to call it fate. I am not sure it is. As a Catholic, I understand that God plays a hand in everything in my life – nothing can happen without his knowledge but when we choose to go against his will, stuff happens that may not be good.

For those of you with other religious beliefs or no beliefs, I advise you to consider that there are times in your life that we did not choose and they do happen. Now, in my opinion, they happen for a reason whether we understand it or not (call it fate or God's will or whatever you choose to call it) but based on what's happened (good or bad), the most effective approach is to accept the situation at hand, analyze your options, and figure a way to move forward. I propose you do not ever waste time worrying or wondering why or how something happened. It just did. Move on.

There have been a few situations in the past 15 years where I have mentored young adults who explained to me that they had terrible home situations when they were growing up (parents who had no interest in their lives offering no guidance, lived in poverty, verbal abuse, etc.). If this is similar to where you find yourself, I offer the following advice: while I imagine this is challenging and frustrating and hurtful, etc., it was not within their control. It is the past. Do not look back, but instead look forward to figuring out what you want to accomplish. To spend precious time trying to understand why you were born where you were born, to whom you were born is likely to result in more anger or other emotions. It is unlikely to provide any answers that will be helpful to you moving forward.

It is equal to trying to understand why we possess a specific skill or talent or why we were given certain talents that others may not have is not productive. It confines you. Some people in life will choose to fight this inevitable situation. Others will argue that since fate dealt them a bad hand and life is simply not fair, they cannot do anything to change it. This is a victim mentality. These individuals are seeking an excuse for not being able to attain their dreams, etc. I would propose you never buy into this way of thinking. Accept fate (bad or good) and then, based on faith, grace, and your choices, plan your life. Embrace moving forward. Do not waste precious time trying to figure out what you have no control over. Life is too short to intentionally put unnecessary stress in your life.

Let's face it. The fact that you are an American is already an advantage. IF you were born in America, even a bigger advantage. Take it from someone who has lived in and/or visited many countries, we are all fortunate to be Americans. America is a great country – consider the extreme hardship others face being born in other countries. Why do you think so many others want to come to our country? We are the land of the free with a tremendous amount of opportunity. Start with this mindset.

Moving forward, take inventory of your current situation beginning with the things that *are in your control*. Decide how you will move forward beyond the things you cannot control. It is important to understand your current state prior to creating a future plan. Acceptance of fate is a significant fundamental in achieving your future because understanding and coming to terms with things you cannot control allows you to begin your journey forward.

In my life, example of God's will or fate was that I was born in Montgomery in 1964. There was no controlling the fact that I was to be born to a first generation Italian-American father and a Polish-American mother. My dad was in the Air Force and mom was a stay at home mom with four children. Thus, my childhood consisted of a very modest upbringing with a lot of moving. This is my story. I had no impact nor control as a child.

Having lived overseas and in many states, I quickly learned that there were other families who were not as fortunate as our family and other families who were better off than my family. But here is an early lesson I learned: appearances are often not as accurate as they may seem. No one knows for sure if the family living in a much larger house or driving a much nicer car is a reality or not (behind the scenes).

As I grew up and lived in many parts of the country, I came to learn and accept that my perceptions of others' lives were simply my perceptions. They may or may not have been reality.

Learning this lesson was important because I realized it was not rational nor prudent to compare my life with others. It was not beneficial in any way to try and keep up with the Joneses. I realized that none of us were actually created equally, we were created uniquely (even if we are twins). For example, I can't sing if my life depended on it so, I did not choose singing as a career.

I promise you; it is not accountable thinking to try and fix the past. Before closing this chapter, I will say while it is important to understand and accept fate (for me, God's will), it is equally important not to use it as an excuse or expect that your talent gives you any special advantage over anyone else. Just accept who you are and always try to improve yourself and maximize what you were given. Your future state, to an extent, is where you have the most control.

What I call the unaccountable loop happens when individuals embrace this mindset: "its fate that I live in this (dangerous) community" or "its fate that I am in this (dead end) job". They say this when they are NOT at all happy in either the neighborhood or the job. This is not fate, this is choice. We have freewill. I challenge this thinking. This is not their fate because they can change by making a choice to get out of the neighborhood and leave the job. BOTH can be changed. Notice you didn't see that I am telling you it is necessarily easy; just that it can be done.

Overview:

Understand Fate.
Accept fate as the will of a greater power to have pre-determined certain components of your life – ones you cannot control.

Do not worry about the past, concentrate on the future.

Create a plan from understanding your "current state".

Do not confuse fate with choice.

Leverage your talents that you have been given.

FAITH

Whether or not we have faith is in our control. Faith is a complete trust in something or someone. I cannot imagine living without Faith – especially my faith in God. In today's environment when there is so much going on in the world – both good and bad, I would have no explanation for how or why so many things have occurred in my life without Faith. I encourage everyone I know to have faith in a greater power, faith in their abilities as well as to have faith in others. It is empowering.

While it is empowering to have self-confidence, a dose of self-esteem, and grit, I would tell anyone I am mentoring that not having faith or trust in other people makes life a lot more challenging. As a Catholic, I am grateful I grew up always having faith. Knowing that failures will come in life but when they do, you can have the belief (faith and trust) that more good will always come from whatever happened. To realize this is calming. It offers an immediate inner peace that I wouldn't want any fellow American to not experience.

In mentoring others and helping them to accept accountability in their life, I have always found that having faith and trust makes for an easier path. First, trust yourself, and second, find a friend who is willing to hold you accountable (kind of like tough love). You have to be willing to be vulnerable. Each you and your accountability partner can write down want you want to be accountable for and make a commitment to hold each other accountable.

Faith creates a better us. When you have faith or trust in another person and that person has faith and trust in you, we are stronger. We want to help each other to succeed. We do not want to see each other fail. If you really have built that faith and trust, you know you can count on that person to help you to meet the goals you have set. If you have ever been on a diet, you know that dieting with someone else is always easier and results in losing more weight. Same with training for a race.

Pretty much any goal you set, research demonstrates that by both writing it down and having a person who you can trust by your side, you have a much better chance of achieving that goal. Research also demonstrates the power of positive thought and staying away from negative people. The same goes for becoming accountable and staying accountable. So, how do you build faith? How do you know you can trust someone? First and foremost, you need time. Learning and understanding and implementing this fundamental may sound simple but not necessarily easy. It will take discipline because having someone believe in you and you in them builds more faith and trust.

Components of building faith/trust:

1) Clarity

2) Compassion

3) Character

4) Competency

5) Commitment

6) Connection

You can secure clarity by writing down your expectations and your goals. Faith does not just happen – you have to make sure you give it some time to develop. In addition, compassion is important because it is very challenging to walk in someone else's shoes. I know for myself that I had to experience quite a bit of life before I really understood compassion for another person. When I was younger, I thought by giving a donation of money or my clothes was the essence of compassion but as I grew older, I grew to understand that you can build a much deeper faith and trust in others only when you listen much more deeply to that other individual's life journey and really try you best to *walk a mile in their shoes* from their perspective, not yours.

To help them to help themselves based on their abilities, their talents, and their desires, etc. is true compassion. Being authentic will lead to faith and trust quicker than anything else. Character is built, I believe, through the compassion you have for others which also happens when you are committed and connected. You need to be competent in your ability to be connected. Over a series of these connections of displaying your character and your competence, you demonstrate your commitment.

In other words, all of these pillars of Faith and Trust that I have noted are essential. You can not have one without the other and still have the best foundation of faith and trust. Life moves fast. We must find a way to use our talents to accomplish everything we are both called to do and want to do. The time each of us is given is unknown. I implore you to live life by maximizing every moment you have received and refuse to spend any time wasting it – especially on negativity. Being able to develop faith (trust in someone or something) is important. Be authentic in everything you do.

To become an accountable person, you need to build some faith and trust. Believe in yourself and your abilities and believe in someone or something else. It is most definitely harder to go it alone. Accountability is more easily achieved by being authentic in building faith and trust.

GRACE

There are two ways to accept grace – one is divine Grace (grace from God) and the other is courteous goodwill. I believe both exists in our country today. As a Catholic, I definitely believe in a divine influence in our life but if you do not, I would implore you to believe in goodwill. To be accountable for oneself entails living intentionally. As you might imagine, when you are intentional, you have to have a plan. I would suggest that your plan includes being compassionate and civil to others. We already have too much polarization in our country today.

If you are going to embrace Grace, you must do so with intention and if you are going to truly live with intention – let your intentions only be positive. There are many Americans who are uncivil to other Americans just because… (you can fill in the blank as there are many "excuses" people use). If you truly want to be accountable, accountability demands compassion and civility. As I noted earlier in building faith, we must be able to demonstrate compassion for our fellow Americans.

We must understand each other's perspectives. I am not saying we must always all agree – that's not realistic as we are most proud of being diverse and sharing differing opinions – but as accountable Americans, we must show compassion. If you didn't know, the word civility is derived from a Latin word meaning citizen. Hopefully, you are starting to see the connection between being the best American citizen you can be – which is to be accountable – which means you accept living with intention.

CHOICE

This is where all your planning comes together! As I mentioned earlier, I look at Fate, Faith, and Grace as the pillars under the roof of choice. If I had to point to one of the most important competencies you should try to hone and add to the toolbox used in life, it would be how to choose. This one ability can help guide you down your life path much more smoothly. Knowing what is behind the HOW and WHY you make choices is critical. In my life, thankfully, the majority of my choices have resulted in more positive outcomes than negative ones.

These positive outcomes have benefitted me and my family and loved ones throughout my life. While this process is not 100% math and science, as evidenced by the underlying factors, the choice part (or freewill) is most definitely controllable. Now, as you might imagine, sometimes even when you mess up in the choice, the outcome turns out fine (this has definitely happened in my life – just pure luck or God's plan) and sometimes you plan and plan and you really make the right choice, and the outcomes are not so good. This is the game of life. It will never be 100% predictable. However, because of your focus on learning, on creating a process or methodology of how to make choices, you can increase your shot at success.

Take your time to perform the necessary research before making a choice increases the potential for a positive outcome (I like to believe). Is it a guarantee? As I said earlier, no. Can it be proven to increase chances? Mathematically yes (if you have put in place the right inputs). My advice is never turn down the opportunity to listen to parents or other grandparents or friends who have your best interest at heart. My belief is that they were put on earth to help guide us, but it is up to use to gain from their wisdom.

<u>Personal note:</u> Family and friends like to tease me claiming that I was born as a middle-aged adult because of my strong inclination to plan, consider, and weigh all my potential outcomes from a very young age. Joking aside, when I was young, I believe it likely comes down to personality traits and preferences combined with support from others. It takes time to establish a plan and execute that plan. There is no magic. Each of us has traits that we like, or we don't. Each of us have things we are good at or that we are bad at. The key is to know yourself.

When coaching others, consider asking 10 questions:

1. What is it that you value?
2. What are your talents?
3. What's your plan?
4. Is it written down?
5. Where are you today in your journey?
6. How do you define success?
7. How far down the road are you looking?
8. What is your backup plan?
9. Do you have a method of how you make your choices?
10. How are you measuring your progress?

Can you answer these questions?

A quote that had a big impact on me was the saying "if you fail to plan, plan to fail." It resonated with me so much so that I intended to plan everything I could possibly plan as early as I could so as not to fail. It was only as I was much older did I understand that all the planning in the world is still no guarantee that life goes the way we want. There is a valuable lesson to be learned from failure.

As a reminder, we were all born with freewill so we can choose what we want (as adults anyway), when we want. My recommendation: choose to plan. Is that a little too much Type A? Maybe or maybe not. There are a significant number of Americans who would have you believe that the ability to make your own choice is only for those Americans in some special category – but my advice to you is ignore that mindset or it will result in you feeling like you are limited in what you can or can't do. This mindset will have you thinking that achieving your hopes and dreams and goals are a longshot based on an exception, instead of the rule.

It is simply not reality. If we are, as a nation, to have a very non-emotional factual conversation about CHOICE in America, then, the fact is for well over the majority of adults (those over age of 17 – at least those Americans born in the end of the 20th century and most definitely those born in the 21st century) ARE CAPABLE, CAN, and DO willingly make choices every day. Some are good and some are bad.

Example of a potential scenario: before choosing to enter into a sensual relationship, what could happen if both individuals paused to think what could happen to their lives in the next ten years if they move forward? What could be the outcomes? Have they thought about what happens if this choice results in having a baby? Have they planned on caring for a child? Have they planned on how to feed and educate a child through high school? If these same individuals, paused and asked "who else am I impacting other than myself?" or "Is my decision an accountable one?" – my guess is the outcomes of choices could change.

We might have some very different outcomes in our nation, wouldn't we? Without starting a debate, I want to point out the lack of accountability in the argument made by some Americans that we as a nation should not have the expectation that individuals can control their "needs". Sorry, but accountable Americans do have that expectation. These outcomes can be controlled through accountable choices.

This example of *fundamental choice*, assuming that the majority of individuals would rethink their choice (to be accountable), would dramatically change in a positive way many of the negative issues we find ourselves challenged with today as a nation including: the number of fellow Americans on welfare, the significant disadvantage that we create for all babies born to single and/or unmarried parents (statistics range from 15% - 77%) and the number of people living in poverty.

Even without sharing all the detailed (and disheartening) data from thousands of sources (you will can easily find if interested), we know that babies born into households without married parents and babies born and raised in single parent households are beyond doubt at a significant disadvantage over babies born into two parent married households.

As outlined in the metrics section, by addressing the fundamental of choice, we can impact the outcome to be more positive. Babies have a big advantage when born into households with 2 parents who are happily married with college educations and stable careers. I bring this point up because it demonstrates clearly how our individual choices can result in either very negative or very positive outcomes for our country. Please accept that an individual's choice (your choice) is vitally important in contributing to outcomes of not only their (your) future but in the bigger picture, impacts fellow Americans.

When the majority of Americans start intentionally considering the potential future outcomes of their choices – be it one or seven generations ahead, I am 100% confident we can begin to heal our entire country and obtain the peace, prosperity, and enlightenment we deserve for ourselves and for future generations to come. These choices involve attitude, where to live, whether or not to go to high school, which friends they choose to hang around with, whether or not to believe in God and/or go to church, whether or not they engage in activities that have either positive or negative results, and the list is endless. You know and I know that every choice has a consequence – no matter how small.

What I am urging you to understand and to be accountable for is that at some point in your life, whether at age 17 or 40, understand the power of your choice and understand that if you can make significantly more good choices, healthy choices, and positive choices than you do poor, unhealthy, and negative choices, you will have a much better chance of achieving enlightenment, peace, and prosperity.

The method of how and why one chooses is one very important fundamental, that, unfortunately, many Americans don't get taught early enough in life or do not want to accept the responsibility of taking that action because of potential outcomes. If you want to be bitter and find blame, you can go down that path but it is not one that gets you very far. My proposed strategy instead is to assess where you are right now in your life, as a young adult or as a parent or as a more mature adult and start today in developing your process for choosing.

Much like trying to build wealth, the earlier in life we start with a good plan and implement that plan, the more benefits we will likely reap. Know that beyond any doubt, the choices you make in life will impact your journey. Bad choices, unfortunately, can really be hard to overcome but in many cases, depending on the choice, you can still overcome them and make better choices tomorrow. Think about how many stories you have heard where one bad choice has all but ruined a young adult's life – especially when they were on the road to a very bright future. Then, think about the stories where that young adult turned, as the saying goes, lemons into lemonade.

If you are a parent of young children, please draft a game plan for teaching your children critical thinking skills so they will be successful later in life. Learning how to assess choices – thinking far enough down the road of their choices' potential impact is one of the best gifts you can give your children. Pause and think about what our country would really be like IF most Americans had a comprehensive process of considering the outcomes of important life choices before they made them. If they understood how to weigh the potential benefits or pitfalls. While the list on the next page shares my personal way I go about making choices, you will need to develop your own based on who you are, what you value, where you are in your life, etc.

Having a plan and a process and being disciplined in using it for the big decisions is critical. I would not suggest you need this process for choosing what clothes to wear but deciding who to date or who to marry or whether or not you pursue college or not are major life events and worthy of a plan.

When making any important life decision, consider asking:

- How will my choice impact what I value in my life (my relationship with God, my relationship with loved ones, etc.)?

- How does my choice contribute to me achieving my goals?

- Do I have time to contribute if I say yes to this request?

- Based on whatever choice I have before me, am I using my talents that God gave me?

- Will the potential outcomes from my choice positively impact my life?

- Is there a financial impact to my choice? Can I afford such impact?

- What happens if I postpone this choice? What are the pros and cons?

- If I ask 3 others who I trust and love for their input on this issue, would they agree with my choice?

- Are the potential outcomes / impacts of this choice temporary, short term, or long term?

- Are the potential outcomes of this decision harmful to others? Or will they bring good to others?

While we are all unique via the gifts we are given and we are all born (I believe) with the capacity for peace and love, we must still choose how we are going to live our lives – whether we will be accountable or not, etc. We must make millions of choices in a life. When making choices, consider this advice:

Choose to be intentional

Choose to be productive

Choose to contribute in a positive way to humankind

Choose to be reflective of the legacy you want to leave your loved ones and our country

This kind of thinking is what accountability is about. When I am in the process of choosing, I vision the possible outcomes – good and bad. Much like you have heard, especially if you have played sports, to imagine hitting the home run, or imagine the ball going in the basket, etc. You want to imagine what happens next and then, imagine what might even follow that outcome. Remember, the lesson of the Iroquois. How about thinking 7 generations ahead. And you think I am a planner?!

While my life planning process includes a plan for short term goals (up to 1 year), mid-term goals (1 – 5 years), long term goals (5 years – 10 years), and then, real big picture (more than 10 years out) goal, I only concern myself with choices and how to make them for short term goals. With today's fast paced world, I think flexibility in the plan is critical so even though I have a plan, I assure you – it has changed several times!

Finally thought on choice: in the Lean Six Sigma methodology, the very foundation is developing a culture of continuous improvement. To continually focus on the pursuit of perfection is not limited to one's professional career but it works in everyday life too. One of the tools in Lean that I like to use both at work and at home is called PDCA. It is composed of:

P **Plan:** set your objectives and identify your goals that you are wanting to reach

D **Do:** Implement steps to realize your goals

C **Check:** Review your activities and your actions against your objectives and your plan to make sure you are on track

A **Act:** Analyze the outcomes of your process / actions and adjust as needed to make sure you are still on course for achieving success

Using PDCA works along with some of the other efficiency tools. Two others are 5 Whys and Fishbone Analysis. I will not get into the details of all of them here as there are thousands of resources you can access online or in libraries on Lean Six Sigma. They have been very useful in my planning and making choices and I am certain you will find them to give you some good information.

Quick story: When one of our daughters was having a challenge getting to school on time, I actually mapped out the entire current state process with her and what the future state would look like based on choices she could make. The results: it worked at getting her to school on time. Many years later as a young adult, she told me that she will never forget that lesson.

STEPS TOWARD BETTERMENT

Accept fate (bad or good) and then, based on faith, grace, and your choices, plan your life. Embrace moving forward. Our country can always use more Grace.

1. Accept Fate and plan your life – just keep moving forward

2. Faith does not just happen – you have to make sure you give it some time to develop.

3. Embrace Grace

4. Make sure you are living with intention by being compassionate and civil.

5. Don't ever blame others for your choice. Accept the outcome. If negative, learn from it and move forward.

TIPS FOR PARENTS

FOR CHILDREN:

Teach them about how there will be things that happen in life that they cannot control but most of what happens to them, they can make choices to increase the likelihood that they will be successful. Teach them how to plan and execute a plan. While sometimes, even if planned, it does not work out. Teach them not to blame others and teach them to have grace.

FOR YOUNG ADULTS:

Review page 108 with them. Walk through these questions so they can begin to understand how important the choices they make are to the potential outcomes in their life. Teach them about consequences. By age 15 or 16, young adults need to understand that they have the right to choose and that their choices will have consequences – good or bad. In addition, a young adult should be held accountable for their poor choices. If when they are young, they are never held accountable by their parents, they will fail to learn one of life's most important lessons: The path they take is theirs to make! No one else's.

Lesson 5:   Your Mindset

If you are seeking to increase your knowledge and are wanting to be more empowered in order to transform your life, think of your mindset as the engine. As part of developing your mindset, your intention and your attitude are like the battery and gasoline (in no particular order) for that engine. Developing the right mindset is really that critical.

Intention

Intention is what you are committing to for a future state. In other words, intention helps you to focus. It provides clarity. It is like a mini-meditation that helps you to determine where you want to spend our energy. When it comes to being more intentional, try this: when you first wake up, spend a few minutes thinking through what is important to you for this day. Take time to think about where you are going to spend your energy and start getting your mind focused in a positive and grateful way.

Intention guides daily action and through your attitude will help you make the right choices. Starting a day grumpy or tired is not likely to lead to being effective that day. It is an intentional choice to be thankful or ungrateful. Even in very sad situations (death of a loved one), we can still choose intentionally to be happy or sad and most importantly, for purposes of being accountable, we can choose intentional civility or we can intentionally choose to be uncivil.

Our lives move at such a fast pace today that we might let a day slip by and all too often it was wasted because we were not intentional in how we wanted to use our time for that day. Even if putting a sticky note up on your bathroom mirror or in your kitchen that helps remind you of some of what you want to get

"Hardship often prepares an ordinary person for an extraordinary destiny"
– C.S. Lewis
Irish-born scholar, novelist, and author of about 40 books

done – do it. Take small steps to being intentional and soon you will build the habit of being intentional every day.

In addition, in today's very technology driven society, we are too glued to social media. Social media diverts us from being intentional. I find it to be more negative then positive – but it is up to you to control it. My suggestion is we make time for "intention." Beyond sticky notes, another strategy is to write down each month what you want to be more intentional about and put it on your desk or nightstand. You will find yourself getting more done.

Make sure what you are being intentional about is positive. Having positive intent helps changing easier and definitely makes getting to your goals more fun. You can more easily shift the way you think if you are passionate about what needs to get done. Being cynical is all too easy. Many Americans' lives are hectic so it is simple to fall into a negative thought process. It is simple for us to accept that this is the life we are stuck with because inertia is easier than doing something.

It is simpler to just go along in life but I am not convinced this makes anyone happier. Unfortunately, there are a large number of individuals who are unhappy in the career they chose as an example. I believe this is due to the fact that these adults are less intentional which results in more complacency. Complacency happens when you do the same thing day in and day out without too much intent and without focus on where you can bring your talents and feel passionate about your goals. I implore you, take the path less followed because the easiest path to take is most often a more boring path and rarely is the path for sustainable success and happiness.

Attitude

It is said that if you think it, it can happen. I would only add the words "much of the time." The "can do" attitude has been studied quite extensively. From my experience of coaching hundreds of students especially having spent four years in the freshman quad back in my college days, I can say beyond any doubt that the most effective attitude to build and maintain is a positive and opportunistic attitude. Such an attitude allows you to exploit opportunities when they are presented. When I was young, my parents' most often told us that we could do anything we set our mind to and they would also say "he who hesitates loses" and "early bird gets the worm" to motivate us. My sister, who really enjoyed sleeping in, never minded that I was always the one going for the worm.

A similar saying is "early to bed, early to rise, makes a person healthy, wealthy, and wise" is useful in teaching young children to think through the choices they make. All these positive messages are great to hear as a child. I believe they really set the stage for a positive attitude. Never too late to remind yourself or ask your accountability partner to share positive messages. Consider what happens after a few weeks of taking on and truly implementing a new attitude of "I can take on anything". When you are a positive person, people react differently to you.

A positive attitude provides confidence and energy. A negative attitude takes too much energy to keep going and it is not good for our health. From my experience in training, I call tell you that a positive attitude is inspiring to others. Now, I may suggest that if you have a colleague that needs his/her coffee, it's only fair you might want to wait until they have their first cup before being extra cheery; but beyond that, most people appreciate inspirational and happy to grumpy and negative.

Mindset

What is a mindset? How does it impact your ability to be accountable? It is your habits that have been developed from the experience you gained from living life thus far. There are really two kinds of mindsets: Fixed or Growth (also called entrepreneurial). You will find these mindsets are very different. If someone has a fixed mindset, he/she is typically set in their ways. They do not feel they have much to learn. They are not enthusiastic about learning a new way. On the other hand, a growth mindset will allow you to embrace new experiences, seek feedback, learn from mistakes more easily, etc. A growth mindset believes life is likely going to require some change of behavior, but this mindset feels that most change can be good.

Most of you have broken bad habits so you know what I am talking about to say it can be challenging - especially as we get older. And I have learned, as much as I have tried, trying to change a fixed mindset in another person who is not wanting to change is nearly impossible. What I found to be true from my life's experience is that a growth mindset serves you better than a fixed mindset. A growth mindset, sometimes also referred to as an entrepreneurial or infinite mindset, is the best kind of mindset for more readily achieving and sustaining accountability. Such a mindset is formed if you can stretch your beliefs; practice being open to what might be possible. If you recall earlier in the book, I mentioned Lean. The lean methodology is about seeking continuous improvement. If this is your mindset, you have a growth mindset.

A growth mindset is one that readily allows us to create positive habits that build motivation and increase productivity. When your mind is open to looking at something a new way, you will ask more questions. When you ask more questions, you are able to learn more. Intention, attitude, and perspective all contribute to a growth mindset. Facts are important. When you ask questions, always seek the truth as one might argue that being open minded means accepting things that we know is not in the best interest for you, your family, or our country so understand that having a growth mindset does not mean changing fundamental truths.

Developing a growth mindset does not come easy for most people. Remember, we typically do not like change. It is easier to be complacent. Establishing and maintaining a growth mindset means having the ability to consider different options, being open to others' ideas. An opposite mindset from a growth mindset is a fixed mindset. As may be evident in the name, a fixed mindset is rigid – set in complacency. An individual with a fixed mindset assumes that many of our skills are a given; they are fixed and unchangeable. Research demonstrates that one's mindset, in essence the way we think about ourselves and the way we believe life works, profoundly impacts our future and IT CAN be developed.

> *"The only way to end racism is to stop talking about it."*
> *– Morgan Freeman*
> an American actor, director and narrator

The old saying of two minds are better than one proves often to be true – especially in problem solving. How many times have you been stuck trying to solve a puzzle or finding the right word and then, a friend comes along and brainstorms with you? Before you know it, the two of you have solved the issue. It is through collaboration that we can achieve more. In summary, make sure you are intentional, have a positive attitude and develop a growth or infinite mindset. All are key to achieving and maintaining accountability. Having the right mindset aids you on being focused on the possibilities and will prevent complacency from stopping you in achieving your dreams. To be positive, ignore all negative and counterproductive noise that is around you.

STEPS TOWARD BETTERMENT

1. Be intentional as often as you can.

2. A positive attitude will help you get through challenging times and allow you to look to your future.

3. Complacency can sneak up on you if you do not work on maintaining an open mind, a growth mindset.

TIPS FOR PARENTS

FOR CHILDREN:

It is important to teach how important an open mindset (ask questions, think about how to do something differently) is and why it is also important to have a can do attitude vs. a cannot attitude. Example: when my own children were very young, maybe age three, they would start to say "I can't do _____" even before they even tried. My husband and I would say to them that they can do anything they set their minds to do and we would ask if they could re-state their sentence with a positive spin. From I can't ride a two wheel bike to I am trying hard to learn to ride or I am almost able to ride this bike but will need a little more practice. We wanted them to build positive self esteem. Starting with I can't was not the language we wanted them to use.

FOR YOUNG ADULTS:

Teach them how to think outside their comfort zone. Explain why a growth or entrepreneurial mindset can make a big difference in how they learn new things. Teach them to be grateful for what they do have and understand that the more talents they have, the more they should be willing to share those talents with others so as to make a positive difference. My dad used to say to me "standing on the sidelines will never allow you the chance to make the goal."

Lesson 6: Mindfulness and Empathy

Mindfulness is the practice of self-awareness. Empathy is an extension of that awareness beyond one's self. Being accountable is contextual. What you want to ask yourself in order to commit to being accountable is: How are you manifesting your own values and holding yourself accountable? Then, ask yourself, how does what you do result in accountability to others?

Here's an example: Let's say self-care (making time for yourself) is something you value and you want to prioritize it because you are feeling stressed quite often. You would want to practice mindfulness in order to manifest the goal of "practicing self care." When you are asked by colleagues to take on a big project that would involve a significant amount of overtime, being mindful would include you pausing to consider if you have the time, energy, and resources to commit to this project. Remember, your priority was to make more time for yourself so that you were more rested, etc. so, by being mindful, you are being accountable (in this example) for yourself.

Practicing mindfulness is important because it helps you to focus on the important values in your life that helps you maintain accountability to deliver those values. Being mindful is one of the key foundations to accountability because when an individual develops a strong mental wellbeing through his/her own self-awareness, he / she is in a position to be more helpful to others. Much like if your goal is to be charitable by donating money to others, you would not be able to do so if you did not take time to budget correctly so that you would have money left over. If you are living paycheck to paycheck, it is challenging to donate to others.

In order to create this good practice of being mindful, you will want to try to establish some routines; make a conscious effort every day to be self-aware. Through self-awareness, like engaging in self-reflection daily (if just for 5 minutes), you can re-affirm your talents and what you feel most passionate about. From a context of self-accountability, most people have an easier time holding themselves accountable to something they enjoy doing. People are not as accountable trying to complete tasks that are misaligned with their values or talents. The other suggestion I have is finding a partner or friend who is willing to help you be accountable.

Furthermore, individuals who are not self-aware have more difficulty being aware of others (and therefore, are less empathetic) and in a nation full of millions of people, an accountable individual wants to contribute to the better good. If you can learn to be more mindful, and you can determine what you enjoy most while using your talents, then you will be able to maximize your energy to helping others (sharing your value). This is being accountable in action!

Example: Say you tell me that you are someone who likes caring for people but you realize that your strengths are not in understanding science. Knowing this, you would not want to take on a job (where colleagues would expect to hold you accountable) for designing some new medical device to help save someone's life. This would likely not be productive for you nor your employer. Through mindfulness and self-awareness, you would better serve yourself and others by knowing what you have to offer (talents) and doing so in a passionate and accountable manner.

Here are some ways to be more mindful in your life:

* Knowing that you need eight hours sleep, and that you have an important early morning meeting at work, you are mindful to go to bed at a reasonable hour versus going out to party.

* Be present

* Meditate or take time to slow down each day and just think about what you have your day

* Practice patience

* Do not worry about small mistakes; learn from them; move forward

Mindfulness involves acceptance, meaning that we need to pay attention to our thoughts and feelings without judging them—without believing, for instance, that we are right or wrong, but instead mindfulness is simply remaining calm in the moment to think or feel. When we practice mindfulness, our thoughts need to tune into what we're sensing in the present moment rather than rehashing the past or imagining the future.

When you are trying to be accountable, a helpful state of being is acceptance and positivity. In summary: to be mindful and to "know yourself" creates a path forward based on values which can inform your decisions, making it easier to be accountable. Explaining mindfulness can be challenging. Another way to confirm your understanding is for me to explain what it is not. It is not NEGATIVE talk in your head. It is not stressing out and being heedless in your decision making. It is not letting your emotion interfere with your logic.

I encourage anyone trying to embrace being more accountable to push all the noise aside that is in our lives. Push aside anything and anyone who is bringing negativity into your space and just find a quiet place to practice being mindful. Once you learn how to do this, it becomes easier to build it as a good habit. In addition to being mindful, an important essential competency is to be able to demonstrate empathy. Empathy helps you relate to others. It helps you to feel what others might be feeling. So how do mindfulness and empathy play a key role in making sure you implement accountability?

Research demonstrates that the more mindful you are, the more empathetic you are. Empathy is asking questions, listening, and understanding people. The more authentic you are, the more people feel that you understand their perspective. This helps for you to be more effective in accomplishing your goals, delivering value, and makes you a stronger leader.

Perspective

Life is a lot of things but simply put, it is a structure of theories about how we believe things work. Our belief systems enable us to make sense of situations we find ourselves facing. As we go through life, we create perspective. It comes from our experience. You may be familiar with this story: six people are blindfolded and are led into a room with an elephant.

In the room, they are asked to explain what they can feel with their hands as they stretch out their arms in front of the elephant (though they do not know it is an elephant since they are blindfolded). They are asked to state only the "facts". One person states that he feels tough flat material. Another person claims that what she feels is soft and flappy and flat. Another person notes that he feels something round and wet and squishy. And the lesson goes on… The bottom line is that each had their own perspective. All of which were factual for that person, but the other person couldn't believe what they were hearing because it wasn't in their view.

The individuals interpreted the data they had; but a gap clearly existed. Therefore, it is important to gather more information and secure as many facts as we can before making decisions but to understand another person's perspective should be taken into consideration; not dismissed. If you fail to ask questions, you might miss an important piece of information. Also, perspectives can change. And they should change as you gain more information that you can verify to be accurate, etc. based on the decision you are making.

Having the ability to consider not only your perspective but another person's point of view is helpful to becoming accountable. Think about it this way: we just simply have no way to know what another person's life has been like, where they are coming from, what they are going through without empathy, without asking questions, and without considering their perspective.

Having perspective means taking off our set of glasses and putting on our friend's, neighbor's, etc. Just trying to look at something from another way, broadens our mindset. If you only wear your set of glasses, I do not think you can grow as a human. The idea of having the ability to hear different perspectives does not mean there is a right or a wrong.

We just simply cannot see it all from one angle and have the best understanding of a situation or coming up with the very best solution until we consider other options. If you have ever had a complex issue that you were trying to solve, you will find it is more easily solved with a few people involved in group-think versus you trying to do it alone. One of the largest benefits of our country is that we are NOT homogenous. There is a reason God tells us that we are Many and One.

We need to leverage perspectives to create the answer together. When we do this, we get the best result. Now, there is no doubt that there are many times in our work lives where teams have been formed and we have reached an impasse. If you get too many individuals involved in trying to resolve an issue, we will have the opposite effect on efficiency. A good approach to effective decision making is to maintain your perspective and develop the ability to consider others' perspectives but not becoming so fluid that you cannot make a decision.

This is definitely a challenge in our country. Especially in politics and companies with lots of bureaucracy. This is the very reason the term "politically correct" came to be. We have now, as a nation, gone so far to one side of not sharing our real perspective, what we really believe to be true, in fear of alienating someone else. We have strayed away from transparency, from our ability of being direct and honest. Many parents today struggle with what I grew up with: Tough Love.

Form your perspective through your life experience and maintain it through truth as you grow but build the competency of being able to consider other perspectives while not necessarily changing yours unless it makes sense to you because you gained new knowledge. Not developing and owning your own perspective contributes to being unaccountable.

In my travels, I have often asked people where they stand on particular topic, what they really believe, and there are more than a few that say they don't know or don't care or they give an answer and when I ask how they came to that belief, they have no reason. With regards to developing all these building blocks, how do you get started?

One way is to find a mentor and also, an accountability partner. If this is difficult for you, I would suggest that there are so many avenues to learn how to better at any skill. Some will argue, it is lack of education. However, I am not convinced that this is the crux of the problem – the crux of the problem is lack of accountability. Due to the lack of people being held accountable, two adults had a child that they are not educating. We must stop blaming the school systems and the teachers. The most important way to teach perspective and all the foundational building blocks to building accountability comes first and foremost from parenting effectively.

Many Americans start each day waking up, going through a routine including a job that they do not find fulfilling, and they are frustrated. When you add this lack of fulfillment with our daily access to a vast amount of social media, technology, and data that comes from all directions, it is no wonder that our young adults have the highest level of mental health needs of any generation before. The journey to changing and becoming accountable can most definitely be overwhelming at first but if you take it one step at a time, I promise it is very rewarding.

STEPS TOWARD BETTERMENT

1. Remember that mindfulness is a calm approach to considering your thoughts and feelings and embracing the moment.

2. Being mindful will help you identify your passion and your talents.

3. Building empathy for others will result in being more in tune with others and helping to figure out how both of you can contribute to a bigger goal. It is a WIN/WIN.

TIPS FOR PARENTS

FOR CHILDREN:

Teach them how to practice being quiet and calm. Teach them how to build trust with friends through listening well. Teach them that asking questions is a good way to build empathy.

FOR YOUNG ADULTS:

Teach them the difference between sympathy and empathy and explain how being mindful will help them to determine what they value in life. Once they understand their values, they can learn to align those values with their talents.

Lesson 7: Asking better questions

Through all the books, sales seminars, or leadership training sessions, one of the most important lessons I learned is how to ask questions. We were taught here are wrong questions and there are "right" questions. The right questions help you to secure data, truth, and accuracy. These are the answers you should want and the answers you need. In sales, our goal is to understand our client and through the information we glean, provide the best solution. In real everyday life, I apply the approach of asking the right question almost every day. You might consider, that as Americans, we seem to be always selling or always buying.

This means that we should learn the skills of asking better questions to understand and learn how to determine what is true and what is false. You likely know the answer to this question: why do we have two ears and one mouth? To listen twice as much as we talk. It is really important to grasp this concept. Listening is the best conversation and communication tool we have in our toolbox. Trust between the two individuals having a conversation is very important because through trust, we can better understand perspective.

For purposes of relating to accountability, let me explain further on what I mean by "better questions." In seeking to further the process of helping others to become accountable, it is necessary to understand that most of Americans tend to rely on emotion rather than logic for decision making. Whether you want to find the facts on something you heard, read, or watched or you are wanting to better understand a particular topic that someone mentioned, you will want to ensure you are asking questions that either can be clearly answered with scientific data or can be answered without bias. This is where emotion (of the deliverer of the news and your own) can result in not providing you with correct/truthful information if you do not ask questions to clarify.

Case Study: A few years ago, a video was posted to social media and it was the objective of the video to explain (a very divisive topic to begin with) *white privilege* to the viewers of the video. The video begins where a camp director offers an award to the winner of a race. This camp leader asks all the teen camp members to line up on the start line. He then proceeds in asking them questions that resulted in certain teenagers having a significant lead in this race.

From strictly an accountability point of view, I propose that the questions being asked were not effective because they resulted in a negative result for all parties involved. I propose that if a different set of questions were asked, the outcomes of "the race" would have been different and could have taught a positive lesson. Instead of promoting divisiveness, the leader could have chosen to highlight how choices can result in positive outcomes instead of promulgating the idea of an advantage one race has over another.

By asking better questions, the young adults could have answered questions that they could actually impact and the results of the race would have taught them positive outcomes from accountable behavior. If you have not seen the video, you can likely find it online and watch it. Think about the questions that were asked by the leader. Then, come back to this section and allow me to demonstrate the difference when you choose to ask "better questions."

Replace the questions that were asked in the video with the questions below instead:

- Do you have a role model in your life that demonstrates what good choices look like for you?
- Do you have a mom or dad that explains the importance of who you choose for friends in your life?
- Have you been taught responsibility through chores or taking on a part time job?
- Do you respect your grandmother and/or grandfather?
- Have you been taught the importance of staying in school?
- Do you have friends who have good habits and good moral values?
- Do you believe in God?
- Do you have goals for the next 5 years?
- Do you study hard to make good grades in school?
- Do you participate in a sport or play an instrument?

Think about the outcomes of the answers to the questions in the video and consider, did these young adults have any control over how those questions could be answered? Think about all the young adults who are wanting to seek truth without bias of race, age, gender, sexual orientation, etc. Which set of questions are more impactful for the young adults in this race to understand how they can make a difference in their lives as well as the lives of their peers?

Let me be clear on why asking better questions matter:

The questions asked in the video were, in my opinion, not productive or positive. They sought to divide these teens. Therefore, the lesson the leader was wanting to teach likely did not improve the teens' lives. The responses to the questions (most for which they had no control) will have no long-term positive benefit for anyone in this running race. In other words, none of the young adults in this video could feel good about their position in the race. The young adults' races (white, Hispanic, black, etc.) have little to do at all with who is near the finish line nor who is near the back or start line if you believe in accountability. The message, I took from this video, is a LOSE/LOSE scenario.

The camp leader's questions would be more fair and more accountable if they were asked of the parents or grandparents of these young adults. Afterall, it was the consequences of their choices that put their child in this position. What is the relevance to the teen's skin color? The answer should be none.

Regardless of race, we know through historical data and research that choosing to secure a college education (which gives you more opportunities for higher paying jobs) and having a baby when in a committed relationship or married will result in a much higher likelihood of staying out of poverty. There are millions and millions of young and middle age adults of non-white races that are extremely successful in America resulting in 8% of all millionaires being Black Americans, 8% Asian Americans, and 7% Hispanic Americans.

So, to have any conversation that asks non-productive, divisive questions where answers do nothing to inspire people, is not accountable and this is the environment we currently live in – in many parts of country. The reality is that in order for these young adults to be able to move forward, their parents at some point in their own lives, made a choice to remain married or work harder, etc. The fact is that many outcomes have to do with fate, faith, grace, or choice and not to skin color, gender, etc. We need to be teaching accountability.

If a young adult comes to you seeking to better understand accountability and how he/she can best contribute his/her talents to achieve enlightenment, peace, and prosperity in life, and is wondering if his/her race will be what holds them back; tell me honestly, what would you tell them. Is he/she best served with the questions (and visual responses depicted) in the video or the ones I am suggesting?

If you want to embrace and sustain a life of accountability, **ask BETTER QUESTIONS**. Seek and find the whole truth. Get the entire picture. Don't ask unproductive questions. Don't ask questions that seek to divide others. In sales, a golden rule is to be authentic. If all Americans would be more mindful before starting conversations with their fellow Americans, maybe we could be more productive. Having a conversation that is not authentic, where neither party has intent to bring value to the other party is not a conversation worth having.

In more recent years, new ideas and even new words are being created and taught to our young adults. Words I never heard when I was a young adult – words like agitator. An agitator is a person who urges another person to protest or rebel. Learning this, I believe that one cannot be an agitator and be accountable. These two words present a dichotomy. I do not believe in the pursuit of protests or rebellion for no logical reason. I believe in helping others to seek a different perspective and move toward a solution that is good for everyone. Remember, learn to ask better questions to seek truth.

Ask yourself: Is force or violence ever a good solution to long term sustainable positive change?

Some Americans will argue that protests and agitators raise awareness. By raising awareness, change will occur. I will politely disagree. Long term positive sustainable change can come (and has in our past) from peaceful dissent. It comes best when we are not divisive and polarizing. Focus on being collaborative. Listen for perspective. Target positive outcomes for all with the central focus on accountability.

Personally, as an accountable American, I know we are capable of changing our rhetoric in our country. In fact, we only need look back 5 – 6 years before some of the recent movements were "intentionally planned" to cause division and harm in our country. These movements embrace divisive rhetoric like privilege and declared that certain lives matter more than other lives. These movements want some people to feel bad. Make no mistake, it was intentional design by individuals seeking to divide us as a nation. It will be essential to our success in achieving accountability to move away from these conversations and back to unified message. An accountable message.

Hijacking English words to create a new "progressive interpretation" is not helping anyone – least of those who need the most help. I have yet to meet a person who seeks to live an accountable life in the pursuit of enlightenment, peace, and prosperity who also embraces the idea of giving certain individuals special advantage or entitlements due ONLY to their skin color and/or gender or sexual orientation AND wants to place blame on ALL individuals of a certain class for injustices carried out by a minority of bad actors. This is not what an accountable person would do. For someone who wants to succeed in life, who wants to achieve the American dream, I can assure you, believing you are a victim will not help you succeed.

A Look Back in History: The original colonists in America used the word privilege at the time the colonies were founded since the word stemmed from the days when after discovery and exploration, explorers were given "privileges" to establish trading colonies. In other words, charter privileges were given to early American proprietors because of the risk they took. Following independence, the colonists no longer felt the need to reference the privileges of Englishmen. When drafting the Constitution, the framers provided little comment as to what privileges and immunities meant.

From the origins of history, the word privilege was created and interpreted during the days of royalty where there were very distinct classes in England. America didn't adopt the term because from the very founding of our country and our drafting of the Bill of Rights, our founding fathers conveyed that we were all created equal. It is very clear that if you believe in our country's founding principles, and you believe in accountability, then, it would be in conflict to believe that some Americans are born with some advantage or right that others aren't born with which causes them harm they cannot overcome.

It is clear that not all Americans are born in equal homes with equal family situations where everyone has a mom and dad and that they are born into equal financial situations, etc. etc. This obviously can never occur because every human is unique. Every journey is unique. We must accept, as I explained earlier, what we cannot control and we must not focus on our attention of how we were somehow shortchanged in life but instead, leverage the positive and move forward. End of lesson; let's move forward.

As an accountable American, I believe in our Constitution which states all men are created equal and we are endowed by their creator with certain unalienable rights (meaning rights that you are born with and that cannot be surrendered) and I would propose that immediately being told that you are starting out life with some disadvantage is a negative mindset which could be a self-fulfilling prophecy.

STEPS TOWARD BETTERMENT

1. Think diligently about questions you ask so that you will have the information you need for making a decision

2. Do not accept negative rhetoric

3. Always seek the full truth in what you read, listen to, watch

TIPS FOR PARENTS

FOR CHILDREN:

Ask your children open ended questions. Help them to develop hypotheses. Help them as they grow to recognize reasoning fallacies and help them to never fall into the trap of being a victim.

FOR YOUNG ADULTS:

Ensure your young adults know our country's history. Discuss the outcomes of some of the choices they made and ask them if they could have done anything differently. Make sure that they understand how to ask questions and follow up questions to make sure they secure all the information before making a decision.

"Enemies are those people behind the curtain jerking everybody's chains and trying to divide us up by age, by race, by income."
– Dr. Ben Carson
American politician, author, and retired neurosurgeon who serves United States Secretary of Housing and Urban Development

Lesson 8: Success for all: An Accountable American Movement

In order for all of us to succeed as a nation, each of us must embrace the concept that we need an aware, active, and enlightened citizenry. In a free country, I have much appreciation and respect for our rights to free speech. Creating powerful causes that help create positive change is part of free speech. What I, along with many other Americans, would propose is for those individuals creating and implementing these "movements" might want to ensure they are conveying their targeted outcomes in a more positive way. In other words, I believe the real intent of a movement should be created in a way to involve "all of us" playing a role and supporting the cause and not having the appearance that if you are not part of a particular group of individuals then you do not have a role to play.

While this is my perspective I am sharing, I can say that as someone who travels extensively, I have spoken to hundreds of other Americans who feel very similar to me. The movements, and maybe because we have so many different ones going on concurrently, feel negative. While they may have resulted in some positive changes, as a rule, the public has not been made aware of these advancements to humankind. What many of us see and hear about is the ill will, the destruction, and the loss of life many of these movements have caused – more divisiveness, the ruining of lives by rushing to judgement without a fair chance, etc.

As an accountable person, it is critically important to ensure that the actions you take stem from personal consideration of what you value in your life. Realize that some of those choices can have significant impact on others. With all due respect, I would propose that as we each focus more on individual accountability, we take more time to consider what the ripple effect will be on our communities, states, and eventually our nation. If we could consider shifting to an "all of us" mindset movement instead of an "us" vs "them" or "all about me" mindset, we would have a better chance of becoming one America. Again, our founders intended us to be one nation, under God and put the systems in place to helps us to remain indivisible.

The ultimate goal we should each have is to maximize our talents, first individually, and then, collectively as a nation to realize our full potential as social beings to continue our pursuit of happiness. This means knowing yourself and establishing confidence in the value you can share by being accountable. This is what it takes to achieve enlightenment, peace, and prosperity

Can you just imagine what our country would be like if each of us would wake up every morning motivated to contribute? And thankful? Understanding that each of us has unique strengths we should be using? You and I both know action speaks louder than words. Accountability is a simple concept and most people understand what it means. The challenge comes in how each of us follows through, how we implement all the necessary components to build the right mindset, get motivated, and be disciplined.

Inaction will always be much easier. Being negative or cynical is easier but is a choice. I am asking each American to consider the possibility of the outcomes that would come from you, all your loved ones, and all of your friends, neighbors, colleagues, etc. creating a Success for All of Us, wouldn't it make each of our journey more impactful? Wouldn't it be less divisive? We could listen more for understanding of the problem we face, work through the problem in a collaborative way that would establish a process that could be measured to confirm success.

Throughout my career, especially when I was in Human Resources, people have asked me the difference between responsibility and accountability. My thoughts are that responsibility can be shared. It sometimes can be challenging to determine who was to take what action; to pinpoint who needs to contribute more or what went wrong. It is easier to shift responsibility to someone else or something else which results in hard feelings and ambiguity.

I feel to just "be responsible" can be nebulous in many situations. To be accountable is all about each of us as individuals. We cannot give accountability away. We must take ownership and when someone is truly accountable, in principle, their accountability extends to beyond just themselves. If you are accountable, there should be no blaming anyone else.

You can't have accountability without first being responsible. Accountability is measurable. When someone is willing to say "the buck stops with me" and they can demonstrate through metrics to confirm a positive impact – that's accountability. When you are accountable, there should be no concern of someone else having "an advantage" because your mindset is concerned for how you are going to bring your talents and interests and what you value to the table to do your best for yourself and your loved ones, etc.

When our daughters were young, my husband and I explained accountability to them when they first came to us to say "my friend made me do that." We responded by asking them to explain exactly how they were forced to make that choice. How did this other person cause you to go down that route? In most situations in life, as soon as you are old enough to start making significant life choices, you should not feel that you are being forced to do anything that you don't agree to do (understanding that I am not referring to violent crime situations).

The goal of this entire book is to present my theory of accountability with actionable steps that will allow any American to move towards a life of enlightenment, peace and prosperity. Being accountable takes practice and it needs to be sustained. On the next page I define what I think can be achieved by becoming an Accountable American.

Individuals who are enlightened:

- Act mindfully to make choices with the future potential outcomes in mind

- Accept their talents they have been given and use such talents to bring value to others

- Challenge what they know to be wrong so as to ensure that others can have the opportunity to secure enlightenment

- Set a good example for others by demonstrating being accountable

- Explain constructively and with compassion what it means to be more accountable to others (i.e. tough love approach)

- Reduce or eliminate unproductive behavior, negative behavior (waste)

- Seek the truth and facts prior to making decisions

- Value logic, religious tolerance, life, and liberty

- Hold others accountable

- Do not engage in negative dialogue

Individuals who secure peace in their life:

- Know who they are and know what they value

- Are mindful of being respectful to others they engage with

- Believe in more than just "doing no harm" but instead seek to societal friendship and harmony instead of hostility, divisiveness, or violence

- Refuse to engage in protests that do not have a positive goal for the common good for the majority of Americans

- Effectively use their talents to bring value to themselves, their loved ones, their community, and can see the connection to their country

- Follow the golden rule

Someone who lives in prosperity:

- Is achieving what they set out to achieve in their life

- Lives a life free from financial strive allowing them to live with less stress, fear, compromise

- Is healthy in body and soul

- Is seen by others as a happy and positive individual

- Generally has a more open and growth oriented mindset and a positive attitude

- Leans more on logic and reason and facts when making decisions

- Has a positive social network surrounding him/her

- Understands the importance maintaining accountability in his/her life so as to ensure the talents he/she has are being effectively utilized

My final thoughts about the importance of choosing to secure a life of enlightenment, peace, and prosperity for ALL OF US:

Pick any issue that would require utilizing the following traits: character, integrity, trust, honesty, and accountability. Some of our fellow Americans would have you believe there a lot of "gray" in choices. Anyone who has ever met me, knows I am up for challenging anyone who believes that the world is only "gray" and therefore, making life choices are gray.

When it comes to the most significant societal challenges we face as a nation, I believe, the majority of the decisions we face and the decisions we need to ultimately make come down to RIGHT or WRONG. I coach individuals that believing in the more comfortable, easier "world is gray" philosophy results in complacency and poor decision making as you are spending your life "on the fence" or "on the sidelines."

Here is my philosophy: We have only been given one life to live. None of us know how long we will have to live it. We have been given talents and unique characteristics to share with others. We were created to be passionate and get in the game of life – not sit on the sidelines. I am not disputing that there have been times in my life at work when I had to make some choices but due to bureaucracy or other issues (none of which are truly impacted my long term life), the choices were gray in nature and it was more difficult to make them; but the decisions I am referring to are those decisions that you are building your very foundation on – what you value, what you stand for, who you are and what you want your legacy to be.

When it comes to those types of decisions, there is no gray. You either believe in God or you do not, you either will choose to help another human in dire straits or you won't, you either believe lying is ok or you do not, you either believe in freedom for every American or you don't. These decisions are not SIT ON THE FENCE decisions. These choices are very clear if you choose to be accountable. I will always believe, in my life, most choices have a clear right or wrong. It is what I teach. In today's America, the challenge for us who want to be accountable and are accountable is there is a large population of Americans who have not been taught right from wrong or simply do not wish to abide by our laws.

Not making good choices is often the path of least resistance. Sitting on the fence or standing on the sidelines instead of playing the game might be easier but will not result in achieve success (easily anyway). I assure you, much like eating the bag of chips and two pounds of chocolate at one sitting, it is not the best choice for you, your loved ones, or your country in the long run. Being born in America is so much better than being born just about anywhere else in the world. It is my hope that in the coming years, we can resolve our country's challenges by creating and implementing and embracing a *Success for All Movement*. Let's demonstrate through positive accountable action what a democracy can deliver. And then, let's measure those results and share them with the world!

STEPS TOWARD BETTERMENT

1. Seek to do more positive good, not just "do no harm"

2. Seek ways to help lift other people through the actions you take

3. Embrace the philosophy that our forefathers wanted us to understand that we will always be better together standing united vs. being divided

TIPS FOR PARENTS

FOR CHILDREN:

Ask your children to talk about how they can help a friend or ask them to tell you a time when a friend helped them. Ensure that your children problem solve with other children so that they learn to collaborate. Life is really about give/take not win/lose.

FOR YOUNG ADULTS:

Ensure your young adults embrace accountability for all – including themselves and their friends. Role play with them on how they should call out someone who is not being accountable. Teach them that being accountable really stems from character.

Lesson 9: Everyday Accountability

The execution of accountability lies in your hands. So, what does everyday accountability look like? When I stop to consider everything we have going on in our everyday life, it is easy to get worn out. We are moms and dads, we are sisters and brothers, we are aunts and uncles, we are bosses and/or employees, we are husbands and wives, and the list goes on. Most of us have quite full plates. Accountability can easily get overwhelming. As noted earlier, this is why being mindful helps. This is where writing down our goals matter. This is where having an accountability partner can help us do what we know is right to do. Below, I review a few big areas and ask you to consider them in the context of thinking about the impact to the majority of us. For the most part, we have some work ahead of us!

Accountability and Education

Educating our children: Where to begin is a challenge in and of itself but I will start at home. I am not sure I can say exactly when it started happening but somehow, we started pushing the responsibility of educating our children to our teachers. We as parents need to be significantly more accountable to teach our children from the day they are born until they day WE as parents die. It is my opinion that there is no magic age that we can stop learning. We will never have all the wisdom we need. As parents, the accountability lies with us to teach our children to read and write and understand the fundamentals from math to manners.

In educating our children, we need to remember that being an accountable citizen begins as soon as the baby starts walking and talking. As toddlers, you can still learn about respect and the golden rule (do unto others as you would have them do unto you). As you enter young adulthood, while parents should absolutely continue to teach lessons from finance to how to change oil in your car, it becomes your responsibility to begin to educate yourself. Teachers and instructors and mentors can always help to guide you, but always want to learn. It is important that you understand that you should never blame someone else for information you can find – especially in today's America, where the internet is literally in your hands.

Student loan debt: There is no argument that the cost of higher education has risen dramatically. This topic could be addressed in a full book in and of itself. What I want to address is the lack of accountability of taking on student debt unnecessarily. Consider the following: There are an estimated 15 million students going to college. The average cost of two-year community colleges are $10,800.00 per year and the average cost of a four-year college was $24,000.00 per year. An average of 41% of colleges students worked Part Time earning an average of $12,500.00 per year.

In addition, 5% of students received enough in scholarship and grant monies to pay for 90% or more of all college expenses and 20% of all students had 50% or more of their college costs covered. So, where does that leave us? With $1.4 Trillion in student loan debt. How? Many families need to conduct more research and secure more detailed information regarding costs to help their young adults make decisions better. It is unnecessary to go into substantial debt.

While I appreciate the desire to go to the school of your dreams in a far from home location, it is not accountable if you cannot afford it. It is not fiscally responsible to choose to run up $100,000.00 or more in debt when a good education can be secured for much less. Why is the argument being made that a high school graduate today is unable to secure a 4-year degree from a reputable university in any state in our country? It is simply not a fact.

Of the 4,000+ universities and colleges in our country, if the student is willing to work a part-time job, there are several hundred universities that provide affordable education. In addition, there are numerous community colleges that offer free to low tuition costs for individuals who have received a high school diploma or the equivalent but are facing hardship. Research just needs to be pursued. In addition, another option is to consider attending to a community college for two years and transferring to finish a degree. If a student prefers to work PT during the school year, he-/-she could have a full-time summer job and earn half the tuition needed at a community college and earn the other half during the school year; then, transfer to a university to secure a bachelor's degree and leave school with under $20,000.00 in debt. Currently, the national average of student loan debt is around $34,000.00 with the average college graduate's median salary at $50,000.00. It is unnecessary for students to take on more debt than they can afford.

Be more accountable in planning your future. A college degree is good but not if you are taking on a thirty-year commitment to repay it. If you really want to go to a private ivy league school, and you do not have the money study harder, plan earlier, play sports, and secure scholarships because having a national student loan debt that is close to $1.4 Trillion is not accountable!

Accountability and Social Media
When the word accountability comes up in conversations, it almost always involves a comment about our social media platforms. Many of the comments people make to one another on social media are completely VOID of accountability. Especially as we get closer to our elections. People can hide behind the screen of privacy sometimes, but many times people

just feel like they can say what they want when they want wherever they want. Social media posts have become so negative and divisive at times, the companies themselves are policing what is being done on these very platforms to ensure nothing dangerous may come from the dialogues.

It is time that all Americans who regularly use social media platforms take a hard look at what they may be contributing (make sure posts are not negative) or at minimum what they are failing to do to hold others accountable. I have elected to utilize some social media platforms infrequently due to the lack of civility (read: lack of accountability).

I personally recommend taking regular breaks away from such platforms just so you do not get caught up in the divisiveness of the "online world". It is taking us further away from real personal and civil human interactions. Lastly, with regards to social media accountability, make sure that anything you post is actually accurate. It is unaccountable to post untruths. It is unaccountable to pass on stories that can harm peoples' lives that are 100% false. STOP being unaccountable.

Accountability and Fiscal Responsibility

Live within your means. Budgeting is accountable behavior. When you budget well and live within your means, you will have money to spare and less stress. When you are not living paycheck to paycheck, you can give some money to others in need and you can invest. Both giving and investing are accountable. It is a parent's job to teach children about money. If for some reason, you did not have the good fortune of learning this from your mom or dad, then, I highly recommend you find some good books to read about being financially aware. There have been over 100 books written on personal finance in the last

10 years alone. Understanding and valuing money will benefit you in every part of your life.

It is also fiscally responsible to try and pay in cash when you can and not leverage credit cards. Paying 18% - 24% interest is never a good idea. Saving often and starting early in life is the key to building up savings and then, learning to invest will result in financial security.

Accountability in choosing your career

What we always taught our children as they were growing up was to find what they enjoyed most, where they could easily use their talents and skills to deliver value to others and the money would come. What I suggest every person seek is a "well paid hobby." Too few people take this approach and instead they seek careers that pay the most money and find out later that this is just "work" and they are not happy. It is really hard to work in a career for 40 years when you do not enjoy what you do. Our job choice is, in my opinion, the second most important decision you will make behind who you marry.

In addition, once you choose a career, make sure you put in what it takes. Be accountable for your bosses and your colleagues. Show up and give 110%. Have a good attitude. While I have had some interesting bosses in my career (I say this with air quotes), it is always important to try to learn from each one. And as my parents taught me early in my career, grass always tends to look greener – but that may or may not be true. Do your research before job jumping.

Accountability and Friendship

You have heard the saying "birds of a feather…". There is definitely truth to this statement. Who your friends are is extremely important. If you are on a path to seeking to be more accountable, you will choose your friends wisely. As you choose your friends, make sure they share similar values in life.

Make sure that they have a good moral compass. Make sure they will "lift you up" and not keep you down. I assure you there is a "wrong" crowd and a "right" crowd when it comes to who you eat with, go on vacations with, etc. Be accountable and make sure that you associate with others who are accountable.

STEPS TOWARD BETTERMENT

1. Think about all the ways you can build accountability in your everyday life – whether in a conversation on social media or in a conversation with a colleague in a meeting. Pledge to be more accountable in your daily actions.

2. If you are in a position, as a parent, a leader, or another adult mentor role, help younger people to be more accountable. Help via a tough love approach or develop metrics to ensure we are being more accountable in the bigger community.

TIPS FOR PARENTS

FOR CHILDREN:

Play games that teach children to think through their everyday actions and choices. My parents used to play games that had tough life questions where we had to express what we were going to do and why or we played a lot of games that involved understanding history so we came to better understand which political leaders developed certain programs or made particular choices and what the outcomes were.

FOR YOUNG ADULTS:

By the time a young adult is entering their teen years, I believe it is critical that they have expectations that have been set by parents and that they learn to meet or exceed those expectations or their will be consequences. The biggest error we can make as parents is when we fail to set a high bar for our young adults to achieve. When we have no expectations, we set no goals, what exactly do our teens have to strive toward? Accountability, learned through these fundamental lessons, learned a little every day, will be the easiest path forward giving our young adults the best opportunity they have to succeed.

Lesson 10: Putting Accountability to the test

Being accountable is everything I have described thus far. Ultimately, it is choosing to control what you can and not being limited in what you think you can accomplish. When I first heard leaders say "get out of your comfort zone" or "think outside the box", I wasn't sure I understood the purpose. Later on as I grew in my career, I came to understand the concept was to have people not restrict their thinking which I completely embrace! As fast as our country is changing (especially from a technological standpoint), it really is unlikely any of us really can get comfortable. Thus, we likely should plan on "living outside of the box." When you are putting accountability to the test, you will have an open and opportunistic mindset, not a closed or fixed mindset and therefore, you are always want to think outside the box so that you can always continue on your journey. Being accountable is not ever stagnant.

When I think of what it means to learn the lesson on having an open mindset and how to demonstrate being accountable, one of my favorite memories was when our youngest daughter was in pre-school and she was put in timeout. Here is what happened: My husband and I received a call from her preschool informing us that we needed to come to meet with the principal and the teacher. Our daughter would not stay in timeout after she was asked repeatedly to do so. In listening to the teacher explain the problem of Kara's failure to stay in the timeout corner, we turned to our daughter (who was 4 years old) and asked her why she did not listen to her teacher and stay in time out.

Kara proceeded to explain to all of us that the teacher drew an imaginary box that was to be the "TIMEOUT" box for which she was to remain for two minutes. With all of us adults listening intently, the teacher then asked her "if you understood that was

"If it is to be, it's up to me"
- William H. Johnsen

the timeout box, why didn't you stay in it?" Kara then looked at the teacher in a very perplexed manner and said "I did stay in the 'TIMEOUT' box, I just imagined the box to be much larger."

We had to give her credit for her creativity and literally "thinking outside the box" but at the same time, we had to teach her that the teacher's rule was meant for the box the teacher drew (though since it was an imagined line, I still think Kara had a point!).

Lesson: Don't create habits that are so comfortable that you are afraid to change or it will cause you to miss out on achieving some dreams. Imagine the box bigger as you put accountability in action. We have always taught our daughters to dream big. I have found that believing in peer pressure or stress is not helpful in moving forward – instead it seems to provide us excuses or reasons why we didn't achieve our goal. Instead (as noted in earlier chapters) understanding fate, faith, grace and their impact on choosing is more helpful on your journey to accountability.

Much like our accountable forefathers had to rise against the British and say enough is enough, I would propose that rising above the noise and negativity is the best approach to start on the path to becoming accountable or helping others to do so. Not wanting to be accountable is antithetical to the America I know and love. And I am convinced, millions of AMERICANS have this very frustration in common with me. We are tired of anyone seeking to divide us.

If you are in a position of trying to help someone else be more accountable, ask them:

- ❖ When it comes to civility and compassion in America, how are we doing?

- ❖ Do you feel that we are being pitted against each other?

- ❖ Is there too much violence in our country?

- ❖ How about bullying, is it on the rise? Are there people hiding behind a false front on social media?

- ❖ How's our country's and family's frustration level?

- ❖ Have you witnessed friends and families who cannot have a reasonable discussion on topics of importance in our country without fighting?

- ❖ If you have not in the past always chosen to be fully accountable for your actions, are you willing to change?

- ❖ Do you believe you are accountable? In what way?

Once a person is willing to accept full accountability of their current situation and agrees to be accountable for everything they can control for their future, then it seems much easier to commit to compassion, respect, and intentional civility. Accountability becomes a positive habit. You will not give credence to negative messaging. Accountability eliminates divisiveness; and results in better understanding why unity (how from out of many, we can become one) is so foundational to our very existence.

If you embrace being an accountable individual, you will NOT allow our politicians, social media, news media, and any individual (those who want no accountability) to thrive on dividing us. We need to information that shares "the good among Americans." Believe me – there is a lot more good than bad. We have more in common than not in common.

Many of us would like to be able to point to undisputable data that would demonstrate the very fiber of our great nation is at stake but we won't likely ever be able to do so – until it is too late and we are living in it. Here is what I do know from our current state of America: While America is still an incredible country, we are more polarized and more negative and less accountable that I have ever witnessed. The stats of high divorce, more lives lost to opiates, tremendous lives lost to mass violence, and the highest anxiety level among our youth than we have ever experienced before in our history.

I read a recent article which found from a study of thousands of children, their anxiety levels were associated with low social connectedness and high environmental threat. During the study's period over many years, social connectedness decreased because of higher divorce rates, more people living alone, and a decline in trust in other people. A professor friend of mine who researches the connection between the lack of trust and social media interaction found many of the same results – we are quickly becoming a country where we don't know our neighbors and we have no problem spreading negativity on social media (it allows us to hide) and blaming others for our issues. I am calling on each and every American to make a commitment to being more accountable.

Our country was founded and has prospered through accepting accountability. From the beginning, our young country had a culture of being accountable for themselves and each other. The average American in the 1770s had a much more accountable life than we have today. I believe the reason for this is, that as a nation, we had more pride. We had established our independence which took a lot of hard work.

"My Fellow Americans, ask not what your country can do for you, ask what you can do for your country." – John F. Kennedy
35th President of the United States

Americans back then knew all too well the restrictions of England. They fought hard to become a new country so they had to be unified; each had to contribute. We were a much smaller country so I imagine that people knew all of their neighbors more personally. To succeed at being accountable, you need to focus on establishing the right mindset. As I mentioned earlier, having a positive, opportunistic or growth mindset means you are open to opportunities. A fixed mindset, as explained earlier, is the opposite – not open to trying new ideas.

Go with the growth mindset – be open to new ideas and learning. Put yourself in the best position to succeed. When you hear comments from colleagues such as there is no need to change something that is not broke or we have always been successful in the past doing it this way, you are hearing a fixed mindset. These individuals have been performing the same job for a long time and are stuck in their ways. To increase your opportunities in securing prosperity, not only in financial wealth but in general happiness, I have found those who are willing to try new things seem to be happier and the happier you are (research data tells us), the healthier you are. It has worked for me. While there are, from a scientific standpoint, some people who can have fixed mindsets and can still be prosperous, I am willing to bet that they are the exception to the rule. When it comes to aiming for enlightenment, peace, and prosperity, I submit that you want to increase the chances of succeeding, not just hope for the exception.

There are few more important times in our life for us to demonstrate accountability than voting. Now, there are two ways we vote in our country that I want to discuss:

1) We vote every day with where we spend our money and
2) We vote in our elections

With regards to where we spend our money, it is unaccountable to support those organizations and/or companies who do not share your values. This is critical to consider because there are many times in your life when you might feel like there is nothing we can do as regular Americans but you have likely heard the saying "follow the money." There is nothing truer.

Money indeed has a voice. Think about Non-GMO foods 35 years ago. Were they available in a grocery store? No. Why not? No one demanded them. Once public interest shifted and the request for Non-GMO foods were sought, they appeared everywhere. Without laws being passed, we can make changes. Wherever you put your attention and your money, that's where we will see change. Another example: many Americans are frustrated with sports stars kneeling at the national anthem. Thus, they boycotted the games resulting in a 6% loss in viewership.

Let's look at social media (which was pretty much non-existent just 15 years ago). Many people want to complain yet 3.8 billion people in the world use social media and the average American spends two hours a day on it. Do you think it is going to go away any time soon? The bottom line is that we can vote with our dollar every day. In putting accountability into action, use your hard earned money where your values are being executed, in companies and organizations who are providing for the advancement of other Americans, and consider where the products you are buying are made.

With regards to voting in elections, voting is an important component of being a U.S. citizen. What does accountability look like with regards to voting?

Preparing to vote in an accountable manner might include:

- Considering what you believe our country stands for

- Consider your values in relation to the principles our country was founded on

- Take all steps necessary to identify what you feel are the important metrics, those critical issues that you believe benefit or can harm the majority of Americans from an accountable perspective, and see how you can contribute to the outcomes of these metrics

- Since actions always speak louder than words, study the track records of said candidates to ensure what they say they believe in is in actuality, what they have accomplished. Remember, a leopard does not often change its spots

- Be armed with accurate information to have confidence that you are voting knowing that you have done everything you can do in good conscious to make an informed decision, a logical decision

"Cognito, ergo sum"
(Translation: I think, therefore, I am)
– Rene Descartes
French philosopher, mathematician, and scientist

Before Voting, An Accountable American will know the answer to:

- What actions will this candidate actually take to improve the lives of Americans?

- How will the candidate's actions align with our country's founding principles?

- Does the candidate firmly support our Constitution and have pride in America's exceptionalism?

- Will this candidate hold Americans to being accountable? Especially those Americans who fail to abide by our laws and treat Americans unjustly.

- What resonates with the future you believe will best support the environment we need to become more accountable?

- Will this candidate reduce government bureaucracy and allow the "we the people" to use our talents and hard work to the benefit of all Americans who are willing to join together in collaboration?

Choosing to be informed about the issues that impact all of us is being accountable. Choosing to be responsible with the one vote you possess by taking the process of voting seriously is accountable. Every American should understand the impact each vote has on all aspects of our country from an economic perspective, a humanity perspective, an environmental perspective, and so on.

As you discuss the right to vote with others and you encourage (I hope) others who are eligible to vote to do so, I would propose that you have robust dialogues with them. Challenge each other as to why they are voting for said candidate. We should not fear having open and honest conversations about what we know because it is clear to me that a lot of information is not being shared by our national media. The only fear that all Americans should have is a fear of other Americans voting with lack of accurate and factual information.

The majority of our news outlets today do not always offer facts. More often, they offer biased opinion. It is quite challenging (sad to say) to find the truth about our candidates today. The ad campaigns do not help much. Why is it that campaigns cannot create an ad that simply highlights the accomplishments of the particular candidate and not just be a biased negative infomercial of another candidate's supposed failures? We must do better.

Why are we the people tolerating such unaccountable behavior? According to national research and public poll after public poll, there are many Americans who are eligible to vote who find it perplexing to answer even the most basic of questions about candidates and their platform. All of us have watched television shows where we end up laughing at our fellow Americans who cannot accurately identify the U.S. Vice President, explain the role of Speaker of the House, explain what illegal immigration is or explain what it means to be a sanctuary city. While these television shows provide entertainment for many of us, I find it sad and embarrassing, and you guessed it, unaccountable.

For those of you that know the answers to the questions noted above, thank you. To those of you who are unsure, I suggest there are many books to provide you with accurate answers before you vote. The topic of our country's history and our obligation to vote should never be a laughing matter. Voting is one of the more significant responsibilities we have as U.S. citizens and it should be taken with full accountability. I am perplexed by my fellow Americans who choose not to engage and understand in our country's issues, but will still vote in good conscious. We must resolve this matter. In addition, there is a significant percentage of our population that simply choose not to vote. You may have been in the following all too familiar scenario as I have been lately:

Fellow American: I am not voting because I cannot relate to either candidate.

Me: What is it that the candidates believe in that you cannot support or relate to?

Fellow American: I just think Candidate A is a racist and I think Candidate B is not honest so there is no good choice for the highest office of our land. I am not voting.

Me: May I ask if you would be willing to share with me what your most important values are with regards to making our country better? What is it you want to see happen and why?

I would be happy to hear your thoughts and then, at least direct you to the right information for you to feel more informed so that maybe you will consider voting. It is truly important that ALL Americans engage because it is only when both you and me do this together that we get the positive changes we need and want.

<u>Fellow American</u>: *Accountable action* - Open to my idea and moves forward in a fruitful discussion. *Unaccountable action* - gets angry and claims it is there right to NOT vote as much as my right to vote.

It is understood that the likelihood of a 100% alignment with everything in a candidate's platform agenda is low, if not impossible. Most Americans would agree that the political candidacy is not always necessarily of the highest moral compass. Your candidate vote should not be focused on personal choices for the best personality, their physical look, or the gaffes made during a single debate.

Voting accountably is about doing the right thing for the country. It is not about YOUR hot button or MY hot button, but about OUR country's best interest, based on our deepest principles, based on facts that we can derive from research, based on what our Constitution identifies that we should hold valuable. It is about the principles of freedom and liberty.

In my 36 years of being involved in our country's political process, I have seen or heard just about everything with regards to the good and bad processes and problems we have with our voting system. Clearly, it is not perfect. As a citizen, you have the right NOT to vote; however, from a point of view of accountability, it is unaccountable not to vote but for logical reasons (outlying circumstances that could cause an unfortunate crisis to occur on voting day).

For those citizens who want to debate the difficulty in getting registered to vote, I would like to bring to your attention that the average American **wastes 77 days** per year watching television, so for those truly interested in voting, for those who want to be accountable - it is possible to find one day to register and another day to spend actually voting.

In today's America where, the voting processes (thanks to technology) have gotten much easier than in 1950 or 1980, I am very hopeful that Americans will accept their right and vote. It will always be difficult for me to be able to comprehend what would prevent an Accountable American from exercising their right. For those of you who are not accepting accountability for being engaged as a citizen, I say this with all the compassion in the world, please reconsider.

The founders wanted you to vote. It is important that you share your voice, your hopes, your dreams, and your privilege to do so but it is indeed your choice. I dream of a time in our country where every American of legal age and eligibility will approach voting in an accountable manner which includes conducting the research to deeply understand their candidates' platforms, the potential outcomes of their candidates' decisions for our country, and consider the outcomes for the long term (not just the few years a candidate is in office). I hope that every American only votes WHEN they have secured have a high level of confidence to vote as An Accountable American.

Some final thoughts on our right to vote: While I risk you, the reader, misinterpreting me, I feel it is worth bringing forward the next topic in context of being accountable. Accountable Americans should have concern of Americans who are pushing to cast their vote without whatever proper identification is deemed required by the state in which they live. The desire that some Americans have to push forward the concept that our system suppresses votes especially based on a specific identity is unproven. Every significant state process and federal process that we adhere to as accountable citizens is of the same importance or even less important that the process of voting and NOT one of them does not require proof that you are an eligible U.S. citizen. Arguing otherwise is incomprehensible.

Voter Identification Issue

As of the writing of this book, thirty-six of our states required a form of identification to vote. It is critical to maintain the integrity of our system by ensuring we hold each other accountable to adhere to this law. Accountability includes ensuring you have the right form of identification and follow the legal requirements for your particular city, county, state, etc. to ensure you are entitled to vote and that your vote will count. Being accountable means wanting to protect this valuable right.

It is the one time in our nation that we as Americans elect candidates that we believe represent us. It makes little logic that someone who understands the seriousness and value of voting would consider it an inconvenience to prove he or she is an American. Americans who take pride for our country and considers himself or herself accountable should not have an issue with our voting process.

According to research, over 80% of all Americans own a mobile phone, over 90% already have picture IDs and/or Driver's Licenses. Included in the 10% who do not have identification or driver's licenses are individuals who have forfeited their legal right to vote due to a felony conviction or other reason. In today's America, no American citizen who wants to be accountable should find a significant burden in providing identification.

Instead, let's concentrate on how to help the fewer than the 10% in the thirty six states that need identification, a way to secure it. Being accountable means demanding that everyone who does have the legal right to vote does vote if he or she wants to do so. Accountable Americans have pride in our country and place American interests as their first priority because we live in America.

Every try getting a license with no proof of who you are? How about a passport? How about loans? Grants? Ever tried buying a house without identification? How about getting student aid? Starting grade school? I cannot think of one single situation in my 56 years of living in America where you secure a right or benefit where the majority of individuals do not understand and agree that proof of who you are is fair and valid.

More recently, accountable citizens are more than willing to wear a mask because they understand it is the right thing to do. It was what we were asked to do – to save lives during a pandemic. We understand the concept of showing an identification to buy liquor. We understand and agree with the concept of having some form of identification to fly. Somehow, the only problem we have is when it comes time to vote. Time to stop the debate, don't you think?

With regards to choosing candidates, Americans should have the expectation that our U.S. President and all elected officials will have zero hesitancy when making decisions that U.S. interests take priority. It should go without saying but he/she is employed by us. We need to vote for candidates who believe in and support accountability for all citizens. As all citizens seek equality and justice for ALL Americans, I will remind them that this means taking a tough love approach for those Americans who want to take advantage of our nation's generosity without contributing when they are fully capable of doing so.

We have a tremendous amount of fraud in many of our systems. We need candidates who will address these issues. Embrace the mindset that, in the long run, it is better to teach a person to fish than to fish for the person. Accountable Americans embrace equal access to everything America has to offer and understand that equal access does not always mean equal outcomes. It is simply not possible because each American is unique in their gifts, their values, and their goals; so therefore, the inputs they choose to secure what they value can be different from another American's inputs.

As an American, you have the honor and privilege of voting for men and women who choose to serve our country as a member of the House of Representatives or Senate. Every four years, we elect a President, a Commander in Chief. Our forefathers never intended to create this incredible country with all the blood, sweat, and tears for any American to be frivolous with the power of voting. Our forefathers also never intended for our leaders to make serving our country a career.

As you may recall from history, it was meant to be citizenry leadership where a person would serve for a short period of time and then, go back into society. We need to re-establish term limits because allowing career politicians accepts complacency. Complacency is unaccountable. Research the number of senators and representatives who have been in office for over 20 years. If you are well versed, well prepared, have confidence in your vote, and follow all the processes and laws to cast your vote, I thank you for being accountable and exercising your right.

Below and on the following pages, I share with you some interesting facts I call *Did You Know?*. After reading each of these, pause to ponder the fact(s) you just read and see how you think accountability plays a role in each of these situations. By reading these facts, I am hopeful that each of you can imagine the choices that were made at some point by all parties involved that resulted in the fact being realized in our country. The conclusion I make is that while we are an exceptional country with some exceptional people, we still have our work cut out to make sure we can move to a nation of accountable citizens.

DID YOU KNOW?

In 2018, 10,310,960 Federal arrests were made. 64% of the individuals arrested were non-citizens (of which 40% were illegal immigrants or ¼ of all arrested).

<u>Pause to consider</u>: Do you think choice plays a part in the outcome of the above fact? What do you think accountable Americans can do to have an impact on this outcome?

DID YOU KNOW?

The Naturalization Exam, which is taken by individuals seeking to become American citizens, consists of 100 questions. However, each individual is only asked 10 questions to answer; AND of those 10 questions, they only need to answer 6 correctly.

Additionally: A 60% grade is passing to become a citizen of our great country though it is barely passing at the majority of the schools in our country.

Pause to consider: To become a citizen, you have to answer 6 of a possible 100 questions correctly. Do you feel this process captures the incredible value and benefits of a U.S. citizenship?

DID YOU KNOW?

Most Americans today, if given the Naturalization test, are estimated to pass at a rate of 33%. So, only 1 in 3 given this test, passed. (If you want to try your luck, the full naturalization test can be found at https://myuscis.gov/prep/test/civics)

<u>Pause to consider</u>: *Should more Americans be held accountable to have a better comprehension of their own country's history? What can accountable Americans do to help ensure they do.*

DID YOU KNOW?

That of 139 million U.S. employees, only 1% are paid minimum wage and of those employees, 48% are under the age of 24.

<u>Pause to consider</u>: *When you read this fact, what is it you think about?*

DID YOU KNOW?

Even with the highest wages for hourly workers ($19.67 per hour) and the largest number of billionaires, _____ still has 30% of all welfare recipients in our country.

<u>Pause to consider</u>: *Which state do you think this is?*

DID YOU KNOW?

The 100 longest serving members of Congress were divided among parties as follows:

71 Democrats
29 Republicans

<u>Pause to consider</u>: *Do you think the framers of our Constitution intended for members in our government to serve more than a few years? Do you know why? What are pros and cons?*

DID YOU KNOW?

50% of all members of Congress are millionaires while the average American earns $31,561.49 (who works for who?)

<u>Pause to consider:</u> The average salary earned by a member of Congress is around $175,000.00 vs the $6.00 a day (only when they actually met) our founding fathers received. Do you believe this is a concern in our country?

DID YOU KNOW?

The average median hourly wage for those working full time is $21.00 or $43,680.00 per year.

<u>Pause to consider</u>: Being this is the Median wage, is it a fair salary?

DID YOU KNOW?

In 2018, the average median salary for college graduates was $72,020.00 and college graduates now represent 35% of our population. (rank of 6th in the world of most educated country)

<u>Pause to consider</u>: This is just one person's salary. Married couples where both individuals have college degrees equal about 12% of our nation's workforce. What can accountable Americans do to help others gain access to college?

"Let each citizen remember at the moment he is offering his vote that he is not making a present or compliment to please an individual – or at least that he ought not so to do; but that he is executing one of the most solemn trusts in human society to which he is accountable to God and his country." - *Samuel Adams April 16, 1781*

Founding Father of the United States and a political theorist

Acknowledgements

A big thank you to my husband for the endless hours he put in handling everything I did not have time for when I was working on the book. Also, for all the times he helped me conduct research and provided input on how to re-word what I was trying to say. As my life accountability partner, I won the lottery. Additionally, tremendous support came from my daughters, and from friends (some of which I have been blessed to have in my life for over 50 years). I thank my dear friends and beta readers who are all accountable Americans: Ellen D. Persefield, Khristina D. Lores, Denton Wilson, Christine S. White, Bryan Golden, Shawn P. Mulholland, Parveen Chand, Valerie Myers, Jo Ann Myers, Teresa L. Simpson, Daina, Elliott Mackay.

A special thank you to those of you who shared your American stories and wisdom to help our readers find their own way to embracing accountability: Parveen Chand, Denton Wilson, Elliott Mackay, and Mia McElroy.

Thank you to the team that put this all together from incredible copyeditors to website designers, book cover designers, and printers!

I thank God for all the blessings he has bestowed on me and my family. Due to His Grace and all the wonderful people in my life that have taught me accountability and held me accountable, I have been able to realize all that America has to offer: enlightenment, peace, and prosperity.

The below quotes by two American Presidents truly embody what An Accountable American is all about and what I hope all

Americans will come to embrace. From the bottom of my heart, I am confident that together we cannot fail. We Americans can create a new positive movement for all Americans to join in – for all Americans to put our best effort to becoming accountable so that we can succeed, individually, and together.

> *"A rising tide lifts all boats"*
> *– John F. Kennedy*
> 35th President United States

> *"There is no place on the whole earth except here in America where all sons of man have this chance in life...here alone is human dignity not a dream, but an accomplishment"*
> *– Herbert Hoover*
> 31st President United States

Appendix

Circle of Influence

Scorecard

Who's Who in the American stories

Accountability: The Pandemic and Civil Unrest

November 3, 2020: The Choice

Conclusion

Works Cited

About the Author

Accountable American Stories – who's who

Pg. 63 - Mia McElroy

Pg. 67 - Elliott Mackay

Pg. 71 - Denton Wilson

Pg. 76 - Parveen Chand

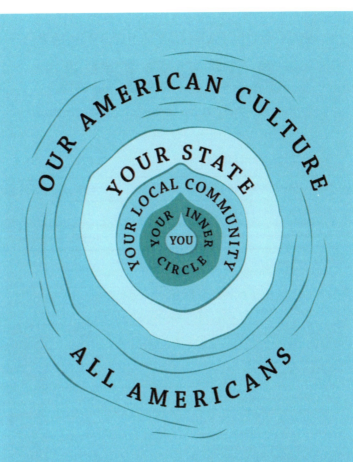

Do you see your level of influence? Looking at this graphic, seek to understand what factors (metrics) could be established, tracked, reviewed, and measured for yourself. Then, for your circle of influence. And continue to build on the accountability path to help your state, and our entire country. If we can start thinking from a metrics perspective about how all of our individual actions (i.e. choices we make), all together, can increase the likelihood for success of our fellow Americans – it would be empowering.

ACCOUNTABILITY SCORECARD
AMERICA
for Achieving a Successful Environment

Significant social factors	1978	2019
% of Married Couples (ages 18 – 34)	59%	29%
% of all babies born to single parent	16%	25%*
% of babies born to unmarried parents	14.8%	40%
% of individuals ages 22 - 34 still living with parents	24%	36%
% of individuals ages <25 with a college degree	25%	35%**
% of households living in poverty	9.6%	13.1%
% of Federal Taxes paid by Top 10% of earners	38%	60%
% of Americans with Health Insurance	78%	91%
% of Americans who believe in God	94%	65%
sub factor: % of Americans attending church service weekly	40%	23%

*By race, the percentages range from a low of 14% (Asian Americans) to 77% (Black Americans) with the majority of single moms on welfare

** While we have seen a rise in being better educated, we are still ranked 13th in the world among all developed countries

Sources: Centers of Disease Control, Pew Research, Brookings, U.S. Census Bureau, Gallup

NOVEMBER 3, 2020: The Choice

Voting is one of the most accountable actions we can take as citizens. Below I am sharing with you the links to both Presidential candidates' websites that outline their priorities. Please, I urge you to read each priority on both platform websites. Dig deeper. Ask the right questions. Hear from the candidates themselves (away from all social media). Make a decision as to which candidate reflects the accountability we need in our country.

Recently, I have heard from many of my fellow Americans. Many Americans share a general lack of enthusiasm for either candidate. We are where we are because we got ourselves in this situation. Being accountable means we must accept where we are, secure the facts, and vote American. What does this mean? It means do not vote only based on being Democrat or Republican. Don't vote on gender or race. I implore you to take your right to vote seriously and vote accountably. Vote in the best interest of all. Remember, it is about ALL of US, not just you.

Based on the fundamental factors in this book and based on a metrics driven approach to securing the best success we can, there is only one more accountable candidate. One that represents doing what is best for all Americans, not just some Americans. One that calls for *Tough Love* and one that will put Americans first, above all others. One that believes that each of us can achieve our dream based on our skills and willingness to participate.

Please refer to each of these websites to understand each candidate's platform

Democratic Platform: https:/joebiden.com/joes-vision/

Republican Platform: https://www.promiseskept.com/

"It is wrong and immoral to seek to escape the consequences of one's acts."

— Mahatma Gandhi
Indian leader of the nationalist movement

Accountability in 2020: The Pandemic and Civil Unrest

There was no way to write a book about accountability and not discuss two of the biggest crises our country has faced in my lifetime: COVID 19 Pandemic and the civil unrest we have witnessed in the past several months. This year, for many Americans, will go down in history as the lost year. In the past 6 months, as I travel still for work, I have spoken to many Americans from every walk of life about both these topics. Our country has experienced a significant loss of life and a crippling economic impact in addition to a severe blow to our mental health with the stay at home orders and civil unrest in many of our states.

Both issues have had an impact on every American. It is incomprehensible that our country along with 95% of the world, in a matter of months, shut down due to this terrible virus. It was a significant undertaking to try and keep as many people safe as possible – without having access to the real facts. Never in my entire life could I imagine this situation – but here we are.

I remember all too well hearing my parents talk about the depression and WWII. I would listen intently and with sadness when they discussed the blackouts they experienced thinking a bomb may hit their home. As a child, I recall the oil embargo (which made finding gas for our car incredibly challenging) and then, there was the Stock Market October 1987 crash. Still by far, in my mind and likely in many Americans' minds, the worst situation we have faced as a nation would be September 11, 2001;

however, even while we panicked and were scared, we came together with our leaders against a common enemy and got through the crisis.

More recently, as I am sure most everyone reading this book remembers, we came through a financial crisis back in 2008. However, within a few years, we recovered, and it did not paralyze our entire country. And while we had some protests, it is still very different from today's landscape. This time is very different because many Americans, beginning with leaders and the media, chose to politicize everything. The result: we have never been more divided, angrier, more hurt, etc. All of these earlier bad times in America are starkly different because not only is a large part of our population at risk from a health perspective and every American impacted from the economic perspective, but the very leaders who we trusted to keep us safe at a very local level, along with thousands of Americans CHOSE to be unaccountable.

Not to mention the fact that we are social creatures who thrive when we are truly united with others. With the pandemic social restrictions, we are prevented from seeing loved ones and from gaining the positive benefits of being around each other. Here we sit faced with mental, physical, and economic pain along with social and political unrest. While some political, business, and community leaders had hard choices to make and did their best to make them, other leaders were working against the very people they promise to support.

<u>The bottom line</u>: COVID 19 is likely to continue as a significant health concern in our nation for some time to

come. This pandemic was not of "our doing" in America – it was not our choice. This is a fact. However, how we choose to react to this situation, to get through this pandemic is 100% your choice and my choice. This is a fact as well. While I can understand and feel the pain and frustration of my fellow Americans who want changes to broken processes and systems in our country, as an accountable American, I am begging all Americans to understand that all the violence and deaths are 100% unacceptable, 100% unaccountable and we own it. There should be ZERO tolerance for what is going on in hundreds of our cities.

At this time, no American in any position has a clear picture of what's still to come. I believe a few years from now, when we look back on 2020, we will realize that politicizing the pandemic and being duped by the inaccurate information being provided by the majority of our media were grave errors. This is why your right to vote is so very important. We must put leaders in place at every level (from our cities and towns to our states and federal government) who are accountable.

Most Americans will never comprehend, myself included, the impact of an estimated $5 Trillion that we added to our country's debt in trying to survive this pandemic. This figure does not include the hundreds of millions of dollars of (as we would describe in Project Management 101) *unnecessary waste* in the destruction of personal and government property along with money spent on resources trying to quell the civil unrest.

The health pandemic seems to have taken a back seat to the civil unrest. Let me ask you this: would our country's environment and culture feel differently if more Americans stood up for accountability? Would our current outcomes been different IF we all just peacefully and accountably fixed our broken processes and broken systems so that we can promulgate justice for all?

Please, choose to be accountable. Use your right to vote. It is the best tool we have right now. Throughout this book, I shared lessons that when learned and implemented can result in positive outcomes. We must understand our baseline, determine what our target goals are, and move forward. It is that simple IF we choose it. To share some perspective with regards to civil unrest and protests in our country, take a look at this data representing the number of violent or uncivil riots and protests that we have incurred in our country over time. These numbers are the TOTAL events during the timelines denoted:

1980's – 7
1990's – 10
2000's – 15
2010 – present – 35

My fellow Americans: This represents a 500% increase in protests and riots in American cities in under two generations. How does a country of such opportunity and such hope create such divisiveness to the level that society has chosen violence as an appropriate response to violence? In just one month, an estimated 100 cities had violent protests resulting in significant injury, looting, and acts of terror and losses of life, property, and economic value in the hundreds of millions of dollars all caused by our own citizens! Does this seem accountable? Not to me. And not to an estimated 50% of the population.

On the positive side of things, the pandemic, while a challenge to all of America, also showed us the good in many people. Our Media, overall, chose, many times to focus on the sensational, so I would like to recognize the positive. I want to thank every healthcare worker, every trucker, every grocery store worker, every local delivery person, every food service worker, and those leaders who worked round the clock to serve the rest of us. I want to thank every police officer, every security and safety officer, every teacher, and all of the hard workers in our hospitals, pharma and manufacturing companies who chose to do the right path and worked endlessly as accountable Americans.

Unfortunately, it is human nature to focus on the bad instead of the good as evidenced when you receive any negative feedback. Many of us understand all too well that the unhappy customer or squeaky wheel gets all the attention and it takes ten good reviews and ten happy customers to overcome the one bad review. Thus, during the pandemic and the protests were reported significantly more than all the good.

Bad actors hijacked the peaceful protests, looting and hurting others. We realize that not everyone is a good person or an accountable person. However, the leaders that hold positions of power have no excuse. These individuals do understand accountability but intentionally chose the path of least resistance and bowed down to unaccountable individuals.

It is my hope that *we the people* who disagree with what America looks like today will use our vote. Just as many of us understand the idea that two wrongs will not make a right; the only real and sustainable way to correct our processes and systems is by voting accountable people into leadership roles and hold them accountable.

During this pandemic, the need for accountability is front and center for all of us. All Americans were called up to step up and to be accountable. We must stand together and commit to empathy and action that will eliminate all divisiveness because it is negatively impacting each of us. The divided country we have allowed to develop slowly over the last 30 or so years is causing 1 out of every 5 younger adults to seek mental health counseling. It is resulting in more obesity, diabetes, heart failure, etc. Not to mention a record number of homicides, suicides, and more.

We Americans have allowed far too many other Americans to be UNACCOUNTABLE. Understand that when you are trying to create positive outcomes, the change process starts with one person but it involves many people to deliver results. The acceptance by the majority of unaccountable action by the minority will only yield more unaccountable actions by these individuals.

CONCLUSION

All lives need to belong to moral inclusion. I have learned in my life that some Americans will have you believe that making changes are impossible; they will tell you that our country has to fundamentally transform because we have so many problems. They will tell you that it is just not likely that you can succeed from sheer desire. I respectfully disagree. When I am asked if the glass is half full or half empty, I respond that the glass is neither, it is overflowing! Our country is a great country and while we have some challenges, it takes but one person with a passionate plea, a plan, and a process and we can create anything we want so long as more accountable Americans join in. Here in America, the process of becoming accountable comes down to a choice.

You must choose to implement a process. Making changes (for most Americans) comes down to *an equation*. The equation, as explained earlier, is the outcome of your inputs – your choices. I hope that the messages, lessons, and stories shared in this book of how to become more accountable resonated with you so much that you embrace and implement these steps to achieve enlightenment, peace, and prosperity. Remember, it is your journey. No one can make you take it.

Your journey will not be the same as mine. Remember, take small steps. Do not get upset if you make a mistake. Realize, everything is not in your control but there is a significant part of your life that is in your control. Find an accountability partner.

May you enjoy the journey and remember, in order to be accountable you will want to accept FATE, maintain FAITH, appreciate the GRACE you receive, and make sure you deliver GRACE when the opportunity presents itself. Accept responsibility for the power of CHOICE, and study history to leverage facts as a foundation to build your road to the future. Keep your eyes on the future. Luck does not often "just happen." It is actually a lot of behind the scenes planning!

Embrace a positive attitude and a growth mindset. Never forget to make time to be mindful and empathetic. Ask the right questions to secure the truth and join in an *All Accountable American Movement* and *Success for All Movement* instead of a movement just for yourself or for any singular group. We each were given one life by our Creator. Live it to do good, bring value, and leave a positive legacy for generations to come. There is only one America. This is OUR America. Let's live our life as accountable Americans to keep the America we know and love to remain the land of the free for the pursuit of life, liberty, and happiness for the next seven generations!

Works Cited

Page 3 – Figures came from: "How Black Lives Matters Reached Every Corner of America" By Audra D. S. Burch, Weiyi Cai, Gabriel Gianordoli, Morrigan McCarthy and Jugal K. Patel 6/13/20
"More than 700 Officers injured in the George Floyd Protests" by Ebony Bowden New York Post 6/9/20
"These are the 13 people who have died since George Floyd protests started last week" *Tim Balk, nydailynews.com. 6/18/20*
"Over 9,000 arrested during days of unrest, as protests continue across US despite curfews". *abc.net 6/23/20*
"Retired officer, ex-college athlete among victims of unrest" *Associated Press. 6/2/20*
"Nearly a dozen deaths tied to continuing unrest in U.S." Aljazeera.com, 6/21/20
"George Floyd Protests Most Expensive Civil Disturbance in US History" William La Juenesse Fox News 6/29/20
https://www.foxnews.com/us/costs-protests-financial-toll-cash-strapped-us-cities

Page 5 – Definitions were taken from Merriam-Webster.com; Lean definition in Wikipedia

Page 8 - Reference MBTI source   onlinepersonalitytests.org Official website is MyersBriggs.org

Page 15 - Definitions were taken from Merriam-Webster.com

Page 17 - Preamble / Goals of Constitution - Public Domain

Page 20 - https://www.bostonteapartyship.com/boston-tea-party-facts#:~:text=No%20one%20died%20during%20the,Dartmouth%2C%20or%20Eleanor%20were%20harmed.&text=He%20was%20the%20only%20person,for%20the%20Boston%20Tea%20Party.
Page 21 - The Atlantic - 6/6/20 article by William J Burns

Page 22 – Fact Checking Sites https://beebom.com/best-fact-checking-websites/
https://mediabiasfactcheck.com/2020/04/12/the-10-best-fact-checking-websites-for-2020/

Page 22 -https://www.brainyquote.com/lists/authors/top-10-walter-cronkite-quotes

Page 31 – Statistics about % married couples, babies born https://www.childtrends.org/wpcontent/uploads/2015/03/75_Births_to_Unmarried_Women.pdf Pew Research, "The Changing Profile of Unmarried Parents." 4/25/2018
Peter Drucker quote https://www.quotes.net/quote/77765

Page 34 – Scorecard data - % of married couples
https://www.statista.com/statistics/183663/number-of-married-couples-in-the-us/
% of single moms and unmarried parents birth data - https://www.brookings.edu/research/an-analysis-of-out-of-wedlock-births-in-the-united-states/
Pew Research "The Changing Profile of Unmarried Parents" – 4/25/2018
Young adults living at home - https://www.cnsnews.com/news/article/terence-p-jeffrey/census-more-americans-18-34-now-live-parents-spouse
College degrees - https://www.statista.com/statistics/184272/educational-attainment-of-college-diploma-or-higher-by-gender/
Poverty-https://www.census.gov/data/tables/time-series/demo/income poverty/historical-poverty-people.html
Taxes - https://taxfoundation.org/summary-of-the-latest-federal-income-tax-data-2020-update/
Health Insurance - https://www.nbcnews.com/politics/politics-news/number-americans-without-health-insurance-rises-1st-time-decade-n1052016
"US Decline in Christianity Continues at a Rapid Pace" Pew research - 10/17/19

Page 34 - % of Americans not paying tax –

https://www.taxpolicycenter.org/taxvox/tcja-increasing-share-households-paying-no-federal-income-tax#:~:text=The%20Tax%20Policy%20Center%20has,percentage%20points%20above%20last%20year.

Page 34 – Single Mom Data - My Safe Harbor post – https://post.ca.gov/portals/0/post_docs/publications/Building%20a%20Career%20Pipeline%20Documents/safe_harbor.pdf | US Census Bureau's 2009-2011 American community survey https://www.urban.org/sites/default/files/publication/65766/2000369-Child-Poverty-and-Adult-Success.pdf

Brookings - 8/10/20 https://www.brookings.edu/research/an-analysis-of-out-of-wedlock-births-in-the-united-states/

"US Decline in Christianity Continues at a Rapid Pace" Pew Research - 10/17/19

Page 38 – Reference to Man in the Mirror Song by Michael Jackson https://www.michaeljackson.com/track/man-mirror/

Page 42 – Six Sigma Formula - https://www.isixsigma.com/dictionary/y-fx/

Page 47 - 1979 Harvard MBA Business School Study on Goal Setting https://www.wanderlustworker.com/the-harvard-mba-business-school-study-on-goal-setting/#:~:text=One%20researcher%20debunked%20both%20studies,a%20plan%20for%20their%20attainment.

Page 99 – Statistics come from US Census Bureau's 2009-2011 American community survey

Page 131 - Privilege in history - article in The New Yorker 5/12/14

Page 145 - Statica.com 3/13/20 – 2018 and https://www.usnews.com/education/best-colleges/paying-for-college/articles/paying-for-college-infographic

Page 145 - Huffington Post 8/7/13 - Georgetown study https://cew.georgetown.edu/cew-reports/learnandearn/

Page 146 - Forbes 2/3/20

Page 154 – Social Media - Stanford University Study 5/8/14

Page 157 - Forbes "NFL Losing Viewers At Alarming Rate But Faces Limits On Its Response" by Brian Goff, 10/23/17

Page 162 - Wikipedia "How Much Do We Love TV? Let Us Count the Ways." by John Koblin 6/30/16

Page 164 - Project Vote "Americans with Photo ID: A Breakdown of Demographic Characteristics." by Vanessa M. Perez, Ph.D. 2/17/15
http://www.projectvote.org/blog/new-research-memo-looks-at-who-in-america-has-photo-id/

Page 167 - 171 – References for Did You Know pages
https://www.cbp.gov/newsroom/stats/cbp-enforcement-statistics/criminal-alien-statistics
https://townhall.com/tipsheet/guybenson/2019/08/23/doj-64-percent-of-federal-arrests-last-year-were-of-noncitizens-n2552109
"Fact Check: Homan many millionaires are in Congress compared to the rest of us?" Amy Sherman 1/24/20 – www.wral.com
www.calculateme.com "What Salary equals $21/hour"
https://www.nbcnews.com/news/latino/most-us-would-fail-u-s-citizenship-test-survey-finds-n918961 Most of Us would fail the U.S. Citizenship Test, 10/12/18 by Allyson Escobar
2 of 3 Americans would not pass U.S> Citizenship Test – US News + World by Alexa Lardieri 10/12/18
https://www.bls.gov/opub/reports/minimum-wage/2018/home.htm
https://usafacts.org/articles/minimum-wage-america-how-many-people-are-earning-725-hour/
Minimum Wage in America 9/18/19
https://www.bls.gov/opub/reports/minimum-wage/2018/pdf/home.pdf
March 2019 Report
https://www.governing.com/gov-data/wage-average-median-pay-data-for-states.html
5/3/2017
https://www.ziprecruiter.com/Salaries/What-Is-the-Average-Average-Salary-by-State
https://www.senate.gov/senators/longest_serving_senators.htm
https://thestacker.com/stories/3563/longest-serving-members-congress?page=5

https://history.house.gov/Institution/Seniority/40-Years/
College Grads earn $30,000 a year more than people with just high school degree" Anna Bahney CNN Business 6/6/19

https://www.epi.org/publication/swa-wages-2019/
https://www.forbes.com/sites/cartercoudriet/2020/04/09/the-states-with-the-most-billionaires-2020/#9e51fb3392a0
https://www.city-journal.org/html/california-poverty-capital-15659.html
California Poverty Capital by Kerry Jackson, Winter 2018
Page 182: Wikipedia "List of Riots," n.d., paragraphs 4.8-5.3.1

About the Author

Having graduated 34 years ago from SMU (Go Ponies!), Lisa is a 5 time entrepreneur, three-time published author, has worked for both starts-ups and Fortune 500 companies, and is certified as a Lean Six Sigma Master Blackbelt. In addition, she has secured certifications as a Senior Professional HR and retirement planner, and obtained her broker's license, all while teaching adjunct college courses for twenty years and having two beautiful daughters. When Lisa is not on the road attending conferences or teaching seminars, you can find her at home in SC with Craig, her husband of 31 years, and their two beabulls, Fenway and Wrigley.

Having grown up the 3rd daughter of a career USAF fighter pilot and entrepreneurial dad, and a stay-at-home and co-entrepreneur mom, developing work ethics and discipline was not an option. Imagine life lessons which included learning what you can and cannot eat in a forest if you were to be stranded for ten days (Air Force survival training 101 – MREs, No Tents, Flare guns, etc. - you get the picture). Or, why pretending to be lost while hiding in a bathroom to teach your parents a lesson (because you were upset about being taught the survival training) only to have a bear park his behind in front of the door for two hours is not a good idea – ever! Lesson learned. Move forward.

Christian. American. Wife. Mom. Sister. Friend. Community Leader. Mentor. Instructor. Consultant. Make no mistake, these are not labels - they are priorities. Three words that define her philosophy in life: Accountable, Passionate, and Disciplined. Life presents ups and downs and challenges. It presents us with opportunities and choices. Learn the 8 Fundamentals you need to achieve accountability to realize the American Dream.